Lending Services   552027
Loan Renewals   552028
24hr Renewal Hotline

Please return/renew this item
Thank you for using

Wolverhamptc

D1494557

X0000000116309

Palgrave Study Guides

Authoring a PhD
Career Skills
e-Learning Skills
Effective Communication for
  Arts and Humanities Students
Effective Communication for
  Science and Technology
The Foundations of Research
The Good Supervisor
How to Manage your Arts, Humanities and
  Social Science Degree
How to Manage your Distance and
  Open Learning Course
How to Manage your Postgraduate Course
How to Manage your Science and
  Technology Degree
How to Study Foreign Languages
How to Write Better Essays
Making Sense of Statistics
The Mature Student's Guide to Writing

The Postgraduate Research Handbook
Presentation Skills for Students
The Principles of Writing in Psychology
Professional Writing
Research Using IT
Skills for Success
The Student's Guide to Writing
The Study Skills Handbook (2nd edn)
Study Skills for Speakers of English as
  a Second Language
Studying the Built Environment
Studying Economics
Studying History (2nd edn)
Studying Mathematics and its Applications
Studying Modern Drama (2nd edn)
Studying Physics
Studying Psychology
Teaching Study Skills and Supporting Learning
Work Placements – A Survival Guide for Students
Writing for Engineers

Palgrave Study Guides: Literature

General Editors: John Peck and Martin Coyle

How to Begin Studying English Literature
  (3rd edn)
How to Study a Jane Austen Novel (2nd edn)
How to Study a Charles Dickens Novel
How to Study Chaucer (2nd edn)
How to Study an E. M. Forster Novel
How to Study James Joyce
How to Study Linguistics (2nd edn)

How to Study Modern Poetry
How to Study a Novel (2nd edn)
How to Study a Poet (2nd edn)
How to Study a Renaissance Play
How to Study Romantic Poetry (2nd edn)
How to Study a Shakespeare Play (2nd edn)
How to Study Television
Practical Criticism

HOW TO STUDY
MODERN POETRY

Tony Curtis

palgrave

Published by
PALGRAVE
Houndmills, Basingstoke, Hampshire RG21 6XS and
175 Fifth Avenue, New York, N. Y. 10010
Companies and representatives throughout the world

PALGRAVE is the new global academic imprint of
St. Martin's Press LLC Scholarly and Reference Division and
Palgrave Publishers Ltd (formerly Macmillan Press Ltd).

ISBN 0–333–46729–9

This book is printed on paper suitable for recycling and
made from fully managed and sustained forest sources.

A catalogue record for this book is available
from the British Library.

12 11 10   9
06 05 04

Printed in China

Contents

General editors' preface

EVERYBODY who studies literature, either for an examination or simply for pleasure, experiences the same problem: how to understand and respond to the text. As every student of literature knows, it is perfectly possible to read a book over and over again and yet still feel baffled and at a loss as to what to say about it. One answer to the problem, of course, is to accept someone else's view of the text, but how much more rewarding it would be if you could work out your own critical response to any book you choose or are required to study.

The aim of this series is to help you develop your critical skills by offering practical advice about how to read, understand and analyse literature. Each volume provides you with a clear method of study so that you can see how to set about tackling texts on your own. While the authors of each volume approach the problem in a different way, every book in the series attempts to provide you with some broad ideas about the kind of texts you are likely to be studying and some broad ideas about how to think about literature; each volume then shows you how to apply these ideas in a way which should help you construct your own analysis and interpretation. Unlike most critical books, therefore, the books in this series do not convey someone else's thinking about a text, but encourage you to think about a text for yourself.

Each book is written with an awareness that you are likely to be preparing for an examination, and therefore practical advice is given not only on how to understand and analyse literature, but also on how to organise a written response. Our hope is that although these books are intended to serve a practical purpose, they may also enrich your enjoyment of literature by making you a more confident reader, alert to the interest and pleasure to be derived from literary texts.

John Peck
Martin Coyle

Acknowledgements

The author and publishers wish to thank the following who have kindly given permission for the use of copyright material: Carcanet Press Ltd for 'This is Just to Say' from *The Collected Poems 1909–1939* by William Carlos Williams, edited by A. Walton Litz and C. MacGowan, 1987; and 'The Hare' from *Selected Poems* by Gillian Clarke; Chatto and Windus Ltd for 'Mama Dot Warns Against an Easter Rising' from *Mama Dot* by Fred Aguiar; Collins Publishers for 'A Peasant' by R. S. Thomas; Faber and Faber Ltd for 'Cuba' from *Why Brownlee Left* by Paul Muldoon; 'Death of a Naturalist' by Seamus Heaney from the book of the same name; 'Thrushes' from *Lupercal* by Ted Hughes; and 'The Whitsun Weddings' by Philip Larkin from the book of the same name; David Higham Associates Ltd on behalf of the estate of the author for 'A Refusal to Mourn' from *The Poems* by Dylan Thomas; Olwyn Hughes Literary Agency on behalf of Ted Hughes for 'Daddy' from *Collected Poems* by Sylvia Plath, Faber and Faber. Copyright © 1965, 1981 by Ted Hughes; W. W. Norton & Company, Inc. for 'Aunt Jennifer's Tigers' and 'Translations' from *The Fact of a Doorframe: Poems Selected and New, 1950–1984* by Adrienne Rich. Copyright © 1984 by Adrienne Rich. Copyright © 1975, 1978 by W. W. Norton & Company, Inc. Copyright © 1981 by Adrienne Rich; Oxford University Press for 'Vergissmeinnicht' from *The Complete Poems of Keith Douglas*, edited by Desmond Graham, 1978; Poetry Wales Press for 'Water' from *Selected Poems* by Leslie Norris, 1986; Anthony Sheil Associates Ltd on behalf of the author for 'In the Theatre' by Daniel Abse; Unwin Hyman Ltd for 'All Day it has Rained' by Alun Lewis from *Selected Poems*, eds Hooker and Lewis, Allen and Unwin.

Every effort has been made to trace all the copyright holders, but if any have been inadvertently overlooked the publishers will be pleased to make the necessary arrangement at the first opportunity.

1

Shapes and Puzzles

I

FACED by a modern poem that we haven't seen before, we may begin by posing the question, 'What makes this piece of writing a poem?' The ready answer is an obvious one, especially if you are a student, for the piece of writing will have been called a poem on the examination paper, or in the anthology in which it appears; or it may have been presented in the poetry class – it is Tuesday morning, and we always do poems in our Tuesday class, don't we? And yet, despite those reassuring contexts, both students and general readers time and again find themselves unconvinced that modern poetry really is 'poetry'. Confronted by a 'poem' which does not rhyme, which does not appear to have a regular metre and which therefore does not sound like a 'poem', how are we fully to accept that piece of writing as poetry? It may also be the case that the subject matter of the poem appears to be quite 'unpoetic', or that the tone of the poet or the speaking voice in the poem appears somehow inappropriate. How can we study such poetry with conviction?

None of these problems may concern the student presented with the following piece of writing:

> Shall I compare thee to a Summer's day?
> Thou art more lovely and more temperate:
> Rough winds do shake the darling buds of May,
> And Summer's lease hath all too short a date;   4
> Sometimes too hot the eye of heaven shines,
> And often is his gold complexion dimm'd,
> And every fair from fair sometime declines,
> By chance, or nature's changing course untrim'd;   8

But thy eternal Summer shall not fade,
Nor lose possession of that fair thou ow'st,
Nor shall death brag thou wandr'st in his shade,
When in eternal lines to time thou grow'st.   12
So long as men can breathe or eyes can see,
So long lives this, and this gives life to thee.

There it sits at the beginning of this book. It is immediately distinguished from the writing which precedes it, not because it is written in a different sort of English, but because the reader sees it differently. The initial response is a visual, spatial one.

We expect the printed word to run from one margin, from left to right, until it reaches the other margin. These margins may, of course, vary from book to book. In the main, writers have little or no control over the page size, the quality of paper to be printed on, or the final appearance of the text. Writers do, however, have total control over the length of their sentences, the number of sentences in each paragraph, the number of paragraphs in each chapter. But as I type this text on the green screen of my word-processor I have no firm idea of the final appearance of the book which you are now holding in front of you. I have held other books from the *How to Study Literature* series in front of me, so I certainly have expectations regarding the format of my own contribution, but as I write I have no control over the way in which these sentences will be printed. Certainly, I the order be hope will right I as intended. But, as you see from that mistake, the matter of accuracy is no longer in my hands once the typescript leaves me.

However, I also write as a poet, and in common with the writer of the piece 'Shall I compare thee to a Summer's day?' I am seriously, even passionately, concerned with the physical appearance of my poems on the page. They must be printed in the form in which they were written. Each piece of writing is a poem initially because I *want* it to be a poem. It comes into being as a poem and as no other form of writing. In Chapter 2 I shall illustrate the nature of that process, showing how an idea becomes tangible, a shared thing, by becoming a poem. Here, though, I am going to concentrate on how to start building a critical response to a poem. The first step in this process is to ask the question –

1 *What sort of writing is shaped in front of me?*

Asking this question of 'Shall I compare thee to a Summer's day?' leads us to establish that the piece of writing is certainly 'poem' shaped. It occupies space centrally on the page; it is quite short, comprising just fourteen lines; these lines may or may not be complete sentences; despite that fact, each of these lines begins with a capital letter, giving the text a distinctive appearance. It is as if the writer were flying words like a flag from the pole formed by those capitals.

If someone were to stand at the far end of a room holding in one hand a sheet of paper with 'Shall I compare thee to a Summer's day?' and in the other the page which you are now reading, though you would be unable to 'read' either text, you would be able to distinguish clearly between the two and see that one of the pages was a poem. Poems are 'framed' on the blank page rather as a painting may be framed. The blankness surrounding a poem, that space which has the potential to be filled by the conventional printing of prose, is acting in the same way to focus the attention of the viewer, in this case, the reader.

The next distinguishing signs which appear obvious *to the eye* are those words which end lines and which have the same letters. For example, 'day' and 'May', 'temperate' and 'date'. Of course, almost instantly one 'hears' in one's mind the sounds which confirm the writer's rhyming intention. At that point no reader who has grown up in our Western culture will have any doubts remaining: 'Shall I compare thee to a Summer's day?' can be nothing other than a poem.

But what sort of poem?

Just reading the opening line, one immediately *hears* 'poetry'. 'Shall' and 'thee' place the writing in the past, in a tradition. The fact that the piece begins by posing a question, and then uses no other question mark is perceived before we have need to engage with the subject-matter of the writing. The reader recognises the question, therefore, as rhetorical, requiring no answer from either the reader, or the person addressed by the speaker. That fact establishes the basis of the reader's response to the text. Each reader faced by a text has an immediate need to realise a role for themselves. That involves listening to the poem, to its tone, its character. This leads me on to the next step in building an analysis of a text: I should

2 *Speak the poem to myself.*

Now this may present a difficulty. You may need to listen to the poem in circumstances which are not conducive: say, sitting at an examination desk in an echoing hall where each sigh, each scratch of the pen may appear audible; even sitting at a table in one's own house with other members of the family present. If it is not possible to read the poem out loud, then at least attempt to *sound the poem out in your head.* Try hard to *hear* in your mind the way the poem should sound, the way you would imagine the speaker or narrator of the poem saying these lines there in your presence.

I should stress at this point that a reading of any poem which renders it into a sort of talking metronome will not help the student to enter into the spirit of the poem and therefore into the poem's true intention. Unfortunately, there are generations of poetry readers (and some of them are teachers) who insist on the metronome count approach to sounding out a poem. This would render 'Shall I compare thee to a Summer's day?' thus:

> Shall **I** com**pare** thee **to** a **Summ**er's **day**?
> Thou **art** more **love**ly **and** more **temp**erate:

The style of reading syllables in pairs, with the first unstressed and second stressed or emphasised, has a powerful hold on some readers. This is the way in which students used to 'count' the feet, or beats, the way in which one determined the metre of a poem. That system of reading and counting, so that one spots iambic pentameters, trochees and spondees is a tradition grounded in classical learning and classical rules of poetry writing. These were adopted as unchallenged truths for centuries in English poetry and served usefully to discipline writers of poetry. However, if one simply looks at the opening lines of our first poem, it is clear that such a mechanical emphasis does more to distort and obscure the meaning and feeling of the poem than a reading which tries to honour the spirit, wit and drama of the poem's occasion. Poems should be approached always as the thoughts, perceptions and utterance of real people in their natural speech or as a deliberate variant of that natural speech.

It is sufficient at this stage to respond to the pace of

this poem by recognising or hearing a regular rhythm. 'Shall I compare thee to a Summer's day?' is composed of lines which have, basically, ten syllables. The lines seem to occupy the same space in time and on the page. This fact, combined with the rhyme scheme which we shall consider shortly, means that the poet is very consciously organising, even controlling, emotions through the poem. We need not distract ourselves with any further specialist terms at this stage. If we respond as readers and audience to the human situation of the poem and the feelings of the characters involved then we will be well on the way to constructing a clear and honest personal critical appraisal.

It is unlikely that the reader of 'Shall I compare thee to a Summer's day?' will assume the role of the addressee, the person to whom these words are directly addressed. That role may be one which readers of certain fictions may assume naturally, as in the invitation, 'Dear reader, let me first tell you . . . ', or 'As the reader of this humble offering may be aware . . . '. This last opening line is too obviously personal, too obviously emotional. Only the most desperate and sycophantic of authors would pro-claim that his or her (unknown) reader were 'more lovely and more temperate (than) a Summer's day': no, we as readers of the poem are immediately aware that we are witnessing a proclamation of affection, romantic love, addressed to another. This could, in real life, be embarrassing; and yet this poem, published, and therefore a public thing, cannot be said to have a secretive, modest tone. The speaker (it may or may not be the poet) is in fact flaunting their affections publicly. That attitude, that stance, will prove to be an essential key to our deeper understanding of this poem. We should, though, also note at this early stage that the receiver of this piece of writing, the person we imagine to be before the writer, is not afforded any response in the writing.

Well, who do we imagine this 'fair' person, this possessor of an 'eternal Summer' to be? For we are left to flesh out the object of the writer's attention for ourselves, given the clearly prejudiced and far from 'objective' views of the writer. The language used, the tone of the speech, is hardly that regarded as admissible in a court of law. It is almost certain that, for a complex of reasons, which are a product of our culture and tradition, we shall imagine that person as a woman, and, for reasons produced by the same cultural complex, we shall perceive the writer as a man. Further, we shall probably, from the outset, see the poem as concerned with human love and beauty.

So far, our responses are, on the whole, both predictable and reassuring: the text *looks* like a poem; it *sounds* like a poem in the choice and arrangement of its words; it takes its place fictionally and dramatically in a set of circumstances which we acknowledge as being part of the proper provenance of poetry. Yes, we know that poems are useful in situations which we may find emotionally stressful. How better to express one's love for another whilst preserving a proper physical distance? That distancing effect is, in fact, one of the central properties of formal verse; the structure of the writing itself works to distinguish the text from the intention of mimetic texts, that is texts, which seek to be a direct imitation of life. We may find increasingly that our reading in contemporary poetry may leave us feeling initially insecure because such a formal structuring of the writing is not evident. The lines may not be of a length; they may not rhyme their final words; we may not hear the steady rhythm of the iambic pentameter, that most traditional, and serviceable metre.

But with 'Shall I compare thee to a Summer's day?' before us there is surely no doubt that the writing is of a different age, from a society which is distant from our twentieth century, though not particularly 'foreign' for all that. We can readily engage with the circumstances of the poem: a lover in his passion flatters his mistress by a comparison which is drawn in the opening line only to be proven inadequate to her beauty in the lines which follow. Each aspect of that summer's day is dismissed – from line 2 down to line 8 – and then, with the 'But' of line 9, the positive, unequalled nature of her beauty is extolled to the end of the poem and its fourteenth line. A poem, of course, can be any length, but most of the poems we will be looking at are fairly short and highly patterned. And this brings me to the third step, the third question it is always useful to ask of a poem –

3   *What patterns can I see in the poem?*

Having noted the rhyming words at the end of the lines, we may make a note of their frequency and sequence. By giving each rhyme a letter of the alphabet it is a straightforward task to make a note of the pattern of rhyme. Thus –

day	– *a*
temperate	– *b*
May	– *a*
date	– *b*
shines	– *c*
dimm'd	– *d*
declines	– *c*
untrim'd	– *d*
fade	– *e*
ow'st	– *f*
shade	– *e*
grow'st	– *f*
see	– *g*
thee	– *g*

We may also see that these lines are organised by their rhymes into four quite clear parts, thus –

abab
cdcd
efef
gg

And that the punctuation of the poem, the way in which the poet wishes us to proceed through the poem in certain stages, at a certain pace, is also clear and measured, with a pause at the end of each line:

day?
temperate;
May,
date;

shines,
dimm'd,
declines,
untrim'd;

fade,
ow'st,
shade,
grow'st.

see,
thee.

After the opening lines and that posing of the rhetorical question, the poet proceeds in a very controlled way. He dismisses that initial comparison by pointing out that his mistress is more 'temperate', more constant than a British summer, with its sudden winds and changes of mood, its unpredictable duration. Then, from line 4 down to line 8 and its colon, he shifts his attention to the sun and the way in which that 'eye of heaven' seems to control our days. As Dylan Thomas says in a poem from our century, 'the weather turned around'. In the third grouping of lines, following line 8's colon, down to line 12's full stop, the poet turns his attention again to the object of his love and at once becomes more positive, extolling his mistress's qualities of constancy and the fact that her beauty is not subject to the vagaries of time. Now he employs weightier words such as 'eternal' (twice), 'possession' and 'death'. Line 12, we must note, concludes the single sentence begun by line 2.

This sentence is by the standards of the spoken word or conversation, and by the practice of our contemporary writing, exceptionally long. One of the difficulties which students constantly encounter in their reading of literary texts of previous centuries is that both poets and novelists, from Fielding to Dickens and Conrad, from Shakespeare to Browning, make greater demands of our concentration within single sentences. We might, in fact, in our reading out loud and our 'reading' of significance in this poem, choose to pause quite firmly at those colons and semi-colons. That way we may enable ourselves to follow and absorb the argument of the poem.

For it is an argument which we are being asked to listen to. The opening line's question is rhetorical because the writer employs it to set up the occasion for his thoughts. He proceeds to weigh the advantages of comparisons between her beauty and the most obviously attractive of our seasons. Then, from line 9, his thoughts deepen, and take in the awful threat of death. Images of light and shade, fair and dark, become much more profound in their implications. And yet, as these considerations deepen, the poet's conviction seems to become firmer, finally rooting itself in the last two lines, the third sentence of the poem. The final rhyming couplet represents a break in the pattern of alternate rhymes. More importantly, it signals the conclusion of the argument and of the poem.

Having looked at the poem's patterns, we can now go on to the next step:

4   *Discuss any ambiguities or paradoxes in the poem.*

It should be clear that the ending of this poem has taken us, as it has taken the poet too, further than one could have predicted. We have explored a set of rather conventional comparisons of a woman's beauty with aspects of nature. These have been found wanting, as an inadequate expression of the strength of the poet's feelings. He knows, as we must know, if he is to be truly honest, that a human's physical beauty must change, and fade and, finally, irrevocably, disappear.

How then, can we account for the positive, almost triumphant conclusion of that final sentence, those two rhyming lines coupled by the sound of 'see' and 'thee' so that there seems no need or room for further argument? I think that if we go back into the poem and read it through once more we will realise that the poet has been cleverer, wittier than we might at first have given him credit for. It is not simply the detailed comparisons which have concerned him, it is that the very task which he has set himself, the construction of the poem, is the most profound celebration of his mistress's beauty. The poem becomes not simply a record of one man's love for a woman; it comes to stand as a justification of art, and particularly, the practice of poetry. What has begun in a questioning tone has ended in an unequivocal confirmation. Yes, poetry is worthwhile, though its wit may sometimes pale and falter before the fact of death and the impulse to be fresh in a poet's patterning of language. The impulse has been love, and the craft of the writing the most impressive, convincing protestation of that love.

To fully understand the poem it seems that we must recognise some trickery on the part of the poet. The central purpose of 'Shall I compare thee to a Summer's day?' hinges on an illusion. There are several paradoxes at the centre of the piece. These may be seen as the following: the poet feels that this poem is worth writing and yet acknowledges that it may be prone to staleness in the execution; it is fired by passion, yet has to be controlled if it is to be worked into an object of beauty; it is a means by which the poet may celebrate the beauty of a woman, yet in its struggle and initial failure to satisfy the strength of his feelings the poet seems to have proven to himself, and to his mistress, that his feelings are genuine. Finally, there is the paradox of sharing by publishing such affections of love; the sense that a reader has of being included in the relationship. That feeling of intrusion is one which all readers of poetry and fiction, and all audiences in the theatre must experience. It is the nature of the art form which makes such an intrusion legitimate; the arts welcome us in, though they may occasionally have unusual and perplexing ways of doing that. This, however, leads me on to the final step.

5 *Summarise my responses to the poem.*

'Shall I compare thee to a Summer's day?' is a love poem by Shakespeare. It takes the form of a sonnet: the first eight lines, though not distinguished as an octave, form the first movement of the poem, examining and dismissing the proposition that the poet should flatter his mistress by drawing comparisons between her and Nature. This was already a tired, clichéd practice in his day, a convention which had lost its effect through overuse.

As in the more traditional Petrarchan sonnet, a second movement begins in line 9, and the third quatrain builds more positively towards affirming the poet's conviction that his mistress is, nevertheless, 'eternal'. The pivotal image is that of line 12, 'When in eternal lines to time thou grow'st', for the lines of perspective can also be read as the lines of the poem itself. It is this play on words which resolves the poet's dilemma as a mortal man and as an artist needing to justify his work in the face of mortality.

The division of the sestet (the last six lines) into that quatrain and a concluding couplet enables Shakespeare to neatly 'lock' his argument into place. A poem which has been characterised by the steady dismissal of a range of poetic devices, has triumphed by the force of the poet's wit. Through his creative originality his powerful feelings of love find expression in an appropriate and memorable form. They are embodied in the poem. 'Shall I compare thee to a Summer's day?' is one of those rare places where life and art meet in a completely convincing way.

II

The moment the reader perceives that a text is a poem important considerations are brought to bear on the response. The word 'poetry' is not simply an objectively descriptive one. It has a superlative force. 'Sheer poetry', 'poetry in motion', one might say in response to the sight of a consummate artist of the football pitch or the tennis court. Of course, the ball and the racquet are not the stuff of poetry, but the use of the word 'poetry' seems to express the degree of our admiration for what we see. We reserve the word for special feelings and, therefore, we may feel reluctant to use that term 'poetry' for pieces of writing which seem to fail our expectations of *Poetry*. Let us move on from 'Shall I compare thee to a Summer's day?', written by William Shakespeare in the sixteenth century, to consider another text:

> This is just to say
>
> I have eaten
> the plums
> that were in
> the icebox
>
> and which
> you were probably
> saving
> for breakfast
>
> Forgive me
> they were delicious
> so sweet
> and so cold

Having read this text once, aloud, or 'aloud' in our heads, we may pose exactly the same questions which proved helpful above.

1 *What sort of writing is shaped in front of me?*

Well, the text is again 'poem' shaped. It occupies space centrally on the page; it is quite short, comprising twelve lines, or, thirteen, if one counts the title. The text has four parts: a single line, followed by three groupings of four lines. The title has a capital letter, as does the first word of the last group of four lines. If I am to make sense of this piece of writing I must decide that, in the absence of any mark of punctuation, I shall have to regard the gaps between the groups of words as pauses, though the gap between line 4 (5) and line 5 (6) is less decisive than that between line 8 (9) and line 9 (10), for 'icebox' is linked by 'and', whereas 'breakfast' would seem to be followed by an unseen full stop when one notes the capital 'F' of 'Forgive'.

Some of the problems I've met here may disappear when I read the poem aloud. And, surely, a reading of the poem necessitates, this time, the reading of the title so that it is included in the piece; it has to function as the opening line of the piece. Bearing all that in mind, I shall now

2   *Speak the poem to myself.*

I find that, providing I treat the text as a thing requiring my involvement and attention, I do not have to rush through the piece. The brevity of the lines encourages me to linger over the words. There may have been an effect of the speaker deliberating quite carefully over these words. They may not be obviously 'poetic', but the arrangement of these 'everyday' words seems to be directing the reader closely to their choice and the pace at which the writer employs them.

There is certainly a *mimetic* quality about this piece of writing. It really does sound as if someone has mistakenly eaten another person's breakfast, and wishes to apologise for the oversight. However, that hardly seems cause sufficient to motivate a poem. Love, death, the passions, are surely not at the centre of this piece. It does not obviously answer the expectations which readers surely have of poems. Though I suppose that 'Forgive' is close to being a 'poetic' effect; and the following conjunction of sounds – 'delicious/so sweet', then the harsher 'so cold' – sets up possibilities of taste associations, even a basic sensuality. One finds the mouth beginning to water at those vowel sounds, then to open around the long 'o' of 'cold'. Still, there seems little to progress with at this stage. Perhaps we had better move on to our next question:

3 *What patterns can I see in the poem?*

It has already been noted that the body of the text is arranged in three line-groupings – dare we call them verses? There is certainly no rhyme in the piece. There is a wilful flatness and banality about the diction of the first two groups, though one might want to argue that the final four lines in some way sound distinct, as if they were signalling a change of emphasis, mood, perhaps some other dimension of the message.

'Message' is a very appropriate term for this text, isn't it? The writer might have scribbled this message on a scrap of paper and pinned it to the icebox. 'Icebox' locates the text in North America, too. So, we have a scribbled message left by an American man or woman. They have left it on the kitchen table, perhaps; possibly taped to the refrigerator, or propped against the coffee-pot, having mistakenly eaten another person's breakfast, and wishing to apologise for the oversight. But why does the recording of such a trivial act as eating the plums warrant this printing out as a poem? What is to stop anyone from chopping their shopping list or class notes into a 'poem-shape' and claiming the result as art or literature?

The answer to that question must be, 'Well, there's nothing to stop anyone doing just that, if they choose'. In the early 1980s the Tate Gallery in London included in an exhibition a symmetrical pile of bricks. They were ordinary housebricks, red, uniform and arranged neatly in a rectangular box shape. The response, particularly of the British press, to this exhibit was loud, persistent and somewhat extreme. At this distance, after some years, it is possible to see that Carl André's bricks and the Tate's decision to exhibit them had worked. Finding itself confronted by an 'outrageous' waste of public space and money, by an apparently self-evident squandering of the privileged position which the arts are granted in our society, the general public, its press and media had reacted to the art. They had taken notice. The bricks had provoked and disturbed people into a response, into taking up some position in the controversy.

Art, including literary texts, should surely affect people, and effect some change in society as a whole. It may be that in order to make its point a literary text needs to surprise readers. This can be done by focusing on unusual subjects, dealing with situations and experiences which the readership does not expect from its literature. It can surprise by radically altering the form of the text, the structure usually associated with its particular genre. It can, of course, depart from the norm, the received view of the poem, novel, play, short story in both its subject-matter and its form.

'This is just to say' appears initially to depart from the norm, if that norm may be taken to be poems such as 'Shall I compare thee to a Summer's day?'. It should not therefore be difficult to –

4   *Discuss any ambiguities or paradoxes in the poem.*

While the 'poem' has some of the basic qualities of poetry in the way in which it visually presents itself, it does not appear to satisfy our expectations of poetry in respect of its subject-matter, which seems banal, insignificant. Again, the poem itself does not rhyme – it does not even obey the rules of punctuation. And yet, there it is before us in a poetry book or school anthology. And, to be matter of fact, it does *look* more like a poem than anything else. To resolve such a paradox it may be prudent to suspend our disbelief. If 'This is just to say' *wants* to be a poem, well, why not allow it that claim and read it critically within that framework?

Poetry works by patterning language. This means that poetry works by calling attention to the words themselves. It 'fore-grounds' the words and the manner in which they appear. Now, this is not the case in many other language uses. For example, when we arrive home with our self-assemble chest of drawers from the DIY store we are not concerned with the style of prose employed by the manufacturers in their accompanying instructions. We have a pragmatic demand to make of those instructions. We will almost certainly not welcome any use of language which is unconventional or 'flowery'; we do not expect flourishes of wit. We want clear, concise and logical instructions which we may read, whilst keeping our fingers crossed that no parts are missing. We count the screws, check the glue, unpack and arrange the various parts to check them against the exploded diagram of the chest. Should any of the listed parts be missing, then we will be unable to complete the task. The piece simply will not hold together.

We immediately see that there are 'parts' missing from 'This is just to say', but we should nevertheless proceed, because, unlike that chest of drawers, each poem, each literary text, holds the excitement of discovery for its reader. Modern poetry, unlike modern furniture, may not be mass-produced endlessly and uniformly. It must, rather, work against the charge of mass-production and uniformity. Modern poets often see themselves as having to challenge general prejudices against poetry as a means of expression. They are anxious to prove that poetry is not stale or predictable.

Again, as with 'Shall I compare thee to a Summer's day?', the reader is listening in upon a communication between two people, or, as this is a literary text, two characters. In a sense, the second poem puts us in a more natural position, for we are more likely to come across a note left in a kitchen than to overhear another person's protestation of love. But just as we may feel the beginnings of interest, even intrigue, when we enter another person's room for the first time, so we are naturally drawn to discover more about the context of the note. What does it tell us about the relationship that exists between these two people?

The title/first line seems to be rather off-hand, as if this were a confession of little importance. However, it takes only a little imagination to project a situation and relationship in which that phrase and this note might be of crucial importance. A couple may have argued bitterly about the plums which they had spent that day picking, or the fridge which should have been repaired, or the other's annoying habit of leaving cryptic notes around the house! The writer of the note is certainly leaving the house, so could it be that they are also leaving the relationship? Could the note be a way of saying goodbye? I find that if I am confronted by a piece of writing which appears cryptic, difficult to understand, challenging, then it is always useful to imagine the piece dramatised in a film. By doing that to 'This is just to say' one can suggest a number of possibilities. Certainly, just as a brief comment may take on great significance in a play or film scene, so a banal note put before us in the form or guise of a poem may be suggesting a *sub-text*, a meaning underneath the surface. By responding positively and imaginatively to the ambiguity of a scribbled note in the form of a poem we satisfy that basic need which all human beings have to make sense of things.

Once we have begun to imagine situations in which one person might leave such a note for another, and once we imagine the possibilities that such an action might represent, then we have gone a long way towards removing our doubts about the validity of the piece. The answer is in the very paradox which mixes the apparently banal subject with the apparently literary shape. The only way in which one can make sense of the piece is by responding thus – 'If this piece of writing *wants* to be a poem, then let me take it on those terms and work towards seeing *how* it works as a poem. Then I can come to make a judgement on how *effective* a poem it is.' I may now be ready to

5   *Summarise my responses to the poem.*

I think that 'This is just to say' by the American poet William Carlos Williams is a very good poem. My personal reading of the poem is one which emphasises the humour in the note. I take it to be a love poem, in fact. The way in which the lover follows on that flat, matter-of-fact admission of his (I am a man and, in the absence of any positive evidence to the contrary, I choose to make the writer of the note a man) having eaten the plums. Then that flaunting of the delicious, mouth-watering sensation of the fruit in the mouth – cold and sweet to awaken the palate first thing in the morning, to *bring him to his senses* – I find very effective. That change of tone and mood and intensity signalled by the capital 'F' of 'Forgive', seems to me, in my reading of the poem, to be a teasing act of love that at once underwrites their relationship and at the same time acknowledges the selfishness which all of us have to recognise in others, even those we love.

I can, too, accept the ambiguity of seeing this piece printed before me in a poem shape yet lacking punctuation marks. I take this to be indicative of the informality of the note, and possibly the fact that the writer is hurrying. He is certainly not intending a full love-letter; perhaps none is needed, though the timing of the note, at 'breakfast', and the placing of the note, encourages me to project a situation in which he has left his lover still in bed, and has left the note to be discoverd at breakfast.

There is, of course, no single, definite interpretation of this poem, and we may well have to make a considerable effort to accept that fact. Poetry and the other arts deal with human experiences in a very special way. Many poems, plays, paintings, films and songs do not present a single point of view or a single argument. Unlike a mathematical problem, there may not be an answer to the puzzle set by the poem. As Ernest Hemingway said, 'If you want a message – try Western Union!'. The arts recognise that life and human motivations are complex and often ambiguous. We do not go to them for formulae or slogans; rather, we expect to be entertained, and to learn something further about life by experiencing (albeit gratuitously) more of life than our lives contain, or that we are aware they may contain.

'This is just to say' works to involve us in a situation which may be 'read' in a number of different ways. And that is what we have to do in our lives on a day-to-day basis. We go through life and our dealings with others, from the most casual working day ones to the most passionate and personal relationships, by decoding a sometimes bewildering range of signals. These include body-signs, social behaviour, dress, rituals and sounds, especially language, that most unique facet of our being, the aspect of our humanity which we so often argue distinguishes us from other animals. Literature is the place where we encounter language in its most sophisticated and deliberate form. Poems such as the two we have studied contribute to our experience of the world and our understanding of human behaviour, for I want to argue that both 'Shall I compare thee to a Summer's day?' and 'This is just to say' are love-poems. Further, I want to argue that both poems work at another level – that of questioning and extending the discourse which is poetry. Each poem works to criticise the accepted poetry norm of its day. These poems are not simply telling a story or staging an encounter between characters in order to explore part of the range of human emotions, they are in their form, their structure and diction making a point about poetry writing itself.

'Shall I compare thee to a Summer's day?' is a *sonnet*. Its form has come to be called a *Shakespearean* sonnet, for it was he who developed this sophisticated variant to the standard sonnet. This was usually a love-poem, and usually written by a courtier. The sonnet became very popular in England in the sixteenth century, though poets still looked to Petrarch (1304–74) as the master of the *Italian* sonnet. Its roots lie in the thirteenth century and experiments with 'little songs' or *sonetto*. The Italian poet Guittone of Arrezzo, who died in 1294, was the writer who established its rules – fourteen lines rhyming *abba, abba, cde, cde* and falling into two distinct parts, an *octave* of eight lines and then a concluding *sestet* which markedly develops a resolution or extension of the theme or dilemma of the *octave*.

Of course, you don't have to know all those things to be able to respond to Shakespeare's poem. What is of interest is that the basic form of the sonnet has survived to the present day. There have been changes in the execution of sonnets, notably by Shakespeare and later by Milton, but the length and basic structure have held an attraction for many of the major poets in English – Spenser, Wordsworth, Keats, Hopkins, Wilfred Owen, Robert Lowell, and our contemporaries such as Seamus Heaney and Douglas Dunn. Whenever a poet needs to write a poem, there is a range of traditional forms which they may choose to use, or, of course, choose *not* to use. Forms such as the sonnet and villanelle continue to attract poets because they have in their form a strength, a dynamic into which the poet may tap. It seems that fourteen lines organised into a rhyme scheme suits our language and the lyrical needs of poets in English. If students are seriously and confidently to extend their studies of poetry, they should make themselves familiar with some of these traditional forms and their possible variants.

III

I want to conclude this chapter by introducing another consideration. How does one resolve the fact that poems employing quite distinct styles and poetic strategies may have the same theme, the same message? This is the principle which informs many examination questions involving a 'compare and contrast' task. Such poems are invariably linked by theme and the poets' intentions. Let us look at the following two poems. Remember to read each 'aloud' or aloud to yourself.

AUNT JENNIFER'S TIGERS

Aunt Jennifer's tigers prance across a screen,
Bright topaz denizens of a world of green.
They do not fear the men beneath the tree;
They pace in sleek chivalric certainty.

Aunt Jennifer's fingers fluttering through her wool
Find even the ivory needle hard to pull.
The massive weight of Uncle's wedding band
Sits heavily upon Aunt Jennifer's hand.

When Aunt is dead, her terrified hands will lie
Still ringed with ordeals she was mastered by.
The tigers in the panel that she made
Will go on prancing, proud and unafraid.

TRANSLATIONS

You show me the poems of some woman
my age, or younger
translated from your language

Certain words occur: *enemy, oven, sorrow*
enough to let me know
she's a woman of my time

obsessed

with Love, our subject:
we've trained it like ivy to our walls
baked it like bread in our ovens
worn it like lead on our ankles
watched it through binoculars as if
it were a helicopter
bringing food to our famine
or the satellite
of a hostile power

I begin to see that woman
doing things: stirring rice
ironing a skirt
typing a manuscript till dawn

trying to make a call
from a phonebooth

The phone rings unanswered
in a man's bedroom
she hears him telling someone else
Never mind. She'll get tired.
hears him telling her story to her sister

who becomes her enemy
and will in her own time
light her own way to sorrow

> ignorant of the fact this way of grief
> is shared, unnecessary
> and political

It is reasonably clear that both poems have women at their centre, and in both poems women perform certain tasks. However, it is just as clear that each poem has a completely different form. That observation leads naturally to our first question:

1   *What sort of writing is shaped in front of me?*

The first poem, *Aunt Jennifer's Tigers*, looks symmetrical; there is a clear pattern of three quatrains. Each verse has two rhyming couplets, employing full rhymes – 'screen', 'green'; 'wool', 'pull'; and so on. Progress through the poem is therefore steady and ordered. We shall find it interesting to relate this to the theme and intention of the poem later.

Translations is, by contrast, an apparently unshaped piece of writing. There is no rhyme scheme and the lines are broken into very irregular sections. An extreme example of this is the one-word seventh line, 'obsessed', which splits a long sentence and, apparently, the flow of an argument. Having used the term 'sentence', however, I must immediately clarify the position: this second poem seems to acknowledge some of the conventions of grammatical punctuation, but also to ignore others. Sentences (for we do perceive them here and read them as such) begin with a capital letter, but do not necessarily end with a full-stop. The only time that this latter happens is in the second italicised line when clearly, someone is speaking directly.

At this point we may summarise that in both poems the poet is anxious to guide the reader through the writing and the argument in a very controlled way. We may conclude, too, that in the second poem we are being challenged as readers in a more radical way.

2   *Speak the poem to myself.*

Aunt Jennifer's Tigers looks reassuringly poem-like. But in reading the piece we may encounter some surprising difficulties. The 'Bright topaz denizens' of line 2 is quite a mouthful, isn't it? Some readers may well have some difficulty in understanding those words. Certainly, such choice of words, such diction is undoubtedly 'poetic'. There is, too, a conscious attempt echo of the 'e' and 't' sounds of the opening line – assonance and alliteration. The fourth line is full of wet 's' sounds, (i.e. alliteration) and these, too, can cause some difficulty. There is further alliteration in line 5, 'fingers fluttering'. This gives a light feathery, insubstantial quality to her craft. The alliterative 'p's of the final line are, by contrast, positive and strong as the panel represents the enduring resilience which Jennifer, tragically, is denied.

In reading aloud *Translations* one has to rely very heavily on the line-breaks. In the absence of some of the elements of conventional grammar, the reader must make the most of the signals of intention which the poet does choose to employ. We shall therefore assume that the section gaps are to be given the respect of large pauses, as one would with conventional verse-breaks; even that one-word seventh line, which now, of course, takes on a great significance. We may be assured that this poem wants to comment on women's 'obsession/ with Love', with a capital 'L'. Again, if we trust the poet, we shall surely find that this flouting of convention in punctuation and typographical layout will prove of significance in our considered response to the poem's intention and effect. Women in general, the poem claims (accuses?), are too conscious of 'Love' (as opposed to 'love'?). It is interesting to consider at this point that the conventionally presented *Aunt Jennifer's Tigers* is also describing a woman's 'obsessional' concern, but, in this instance, with her decoration of the panel at which she constantly works.

Finally, we might perceive that the apparently random layout of *Translations* does succeed, particularly in its middle sections, in stressing activities in a detailed list; and that is one of the central impressions one receives of the actions of Aunt Jennifer.

3   *What patterns can I see in the poem?*

Aunt Jennifer's Tigers patterns words by employing a regularity of rhythm as well as in its use of strong rhymes. The lines have a basic rhythm that features five strong stresses, as in

> Aunt **Jenn**ifer's **ti**gers **prance** across a **screen**,
> **Bright to**paz **den**izens of a **world** of **green**.

We may recall that this basis of a ten syllable, five stress line was encountered in the Shakespeare sonnet. The present poet is, then, consciously striving for a form of poetry which accords with traditional notions of pace and rhythm. And why not? The poem concerns a woman who spends hours working on a 'screen' – a fire-screen, perhaps – by decorating it with a woven design of tigers in an exotic jungle scene. What better way to communicate that task than by creating a poem which has a clear discipline in its form and a measured pace? The patterning of rhyme through the three quatrains creates a tightly woven effect. The rhyming couplets measure the poem's progress into six sentences. This is the sort of disciplined writing which one might expect to convey assurance and predictability. Of course, the sense of order and predictability in this poem are at the very centre of the poet's concern. But we shall develop that in our next stage of questioning.

Translations at first appears to have no pattern whatsoever. We have already noted the lack of regular verses and the fact that the sentence formations and typography seem to be unconventional, even random. However, there is the linear structure of the narrative; the encounter with 'some woman/my age, or younger'. This poet, this woman (for she declares herself to be a woman, and it would be perverse for us to see the poem as a man writing *in persona* without strong evidence for that) responds herself to a selection of poems, and through those responses projects the life-style and experiences of another woman, from another culture. But as early as line 6 she is developing a strong empathy with that other woman. The paragraph which follows 'obsessed' has the relentless weight of a list of evidences which broadens the argument that *all* women share a common experience (a common fault?) – that of being seduced and distracted by the desire to be 'loved'. And this is a 'love' which is culturally fixed, even across national divisions. It is possible, then, to see *Translations* as being the development of an argument over three sections –

1 'You show me . . . obsessed'
2 'with Love . . . hostile power'
3 'I begin . . . and political'

First comes the notion of another woman with similar experiences, despite the fact that she is foreign, and requires 'translation';

then there is the listing and examination of the nature of that 'obsession' shared by all women; and, finally, the projection of an instance of that 'obsession', which leads the poet, and, she hopes, her readers, to an anger which realises itself in the shock that such personal issues may be 'shared, unnecessary/ and political'. The pattern of the poem's progress is that of a three-stage argument. We note, too, that it employs repetition of syntax in reiterating the 'obsession' with 'Love'; also, in the reappearance of 'enemy' and 'sorrow' towards the end of the poem a locking together of that argument is intended. There are points in this poem at which the poet is also consciously linking sounds. For example, the internal rhyme of 'bread' and 'lead' in lines 10 and 11; also the triplet of 'stirring rice/ ironing a skirt/ typing a manuscript till dawn' and the groupings of other details in threes – lines 9, 10, 11, and the concluding 'shared, unnecessary/ and political', all these details work towards a sense of patterning which underpins the narrative.

4   *Discuss any ambiguities or paradoxes in the poems.*

The central point to be made in any such exercise of comparison is, of course, the way in which the two poems engage a single issue or similar issues whilst employing distinctive and possibly contrasting poetic means or 'strategies'. *Aunt Jennifer's Tigers* would seem to exemplify 'The Well-Made Poem'. Its disciplined, skilful patterning of words surely complements the actions of the aunt. Her life is outwardly dedicated to the 'womanly' arts; she creates a work of art which decorates a household utensil, a fire-screen. The activity seems dated, the needle is ivory, the screen a period piece. The aunt is a memory from the poet's childhood, no doubt.

But this is not simply an 'affectionate memory', a colourful section of one's autobiography. It is, rather, the later, adult realisation of what precisely the aunt's life held for her, and of the significance of that embroidery in terms of her personality and her marriage. The tigers have a strength and an independence denied to Jennifer, as they 'prance' across her screen. They are 'Bright topaz denizens' – brightly yellow, with the confidence of creatures admitted to a world which they then command as their own. Their 'sleek, chivalric certainty' implies a formal, courtly quality. These creatures of the imagination, of fantasy, are both wild and heraldic, fearing no dominance by Man; unlike cowed, submissive Jennifer anchored by the 'massive weight of Uncle's wedding band'. It is a weight which represents the quiet ordeals of an unequal marriage, a marriage in which her fingers are 'terrified' and in which they have 'fluttered' like caged birds over the laborious task of decorating the screen. Her marriage and the task specified in the poem are never what they seem, or what they should really be. The security of the one and the creativity of the other are negated by the oppression which they represent.

Jennifer is, throughout the poem, characterised by her hands and their activity. We are told nothing of her physical appearance and yet we need to know no more of her nature or spirit beyond that which is so remarkably conveyed by her 'fluttering fingers'. That concentration on one aspect of a person (or a place, or an institution) as a general representation of the whole is termed 'metonomy'. By choosing to concentrate on the hands, and on one activity, *Aunt Jennifer's Tigers* is a notable example of a poem which rests on that device. The poem's apparent narrow frame of reference contains a whole picture, just as the embroidered screen could be said to.

The action and the situation are deeply ambiguous and the poet, Adrienne Rich, writing in 1951, can see clearly the outrage instanced by that solitary woman's entrapment. She writes with an irony, fired by anger. The closing image of the tigers that 'go on prancing, proud and unafraid' is a clarion call, a protest which is ambiguous only because it is just that – an image – and because the energy, anger and possibilities for change which the tigers by now represent have all come too late for her Aunt Jennifer. What is certainly unambiguous is that sense of empathy and the transference of anger and frustration at a life stunted and repressed. Adrienne Rich seems to be calling for real tigers, a tigerish assertion of individual rights for herself and the women of her generation. There is a sense in which this poem is 'political' and in which it demands to be read as 'political' in an age which has seen the beginnings of a radical reassessment of gender roles. Though labels are dangerous devices for literary critics, we might not be risking too much by venturing that *Aunt Jennifer's Tigers* is a feminist poem.

Translations proclaims itself directly to be such a 'feminist' poem. The central ambiguity of this piece is that of its refusal to satisfy traditional notions of what poetry should be. It chooses an alternative aesthetic and follows a form and a logic accordingly. There are just as many levels of meaning and occasions for irony here as in *Aunt Jennifer's Tigers*. *Translations* is a poem which has its roots in another poem. However, it works by moving in style and subject matter away from, and beyond, its starting point. It, in fact, 'translates' one experience into many other experiences: it 'translates' some basic words from one language experience to another; it 'translates' or metamorphoses an abstract 'love' into examples of physical oppression and restraint; it finally 'translates' the entrapment of a woman from one culture to another, Western culture, 'translating' a generalised sense of women's positions to that of a single woman coerced by a single man and ironically taking her 'sister' in womanhood to be her 'enemy' in a love affair.

This is a poem which instances many more examples of 'womanly' activities than *Aunt Jennifer's Tigers*. One might argue that by so doing a certain unity of action and intensity of anger is dissipated. However, there is anger in the poem, particularly in the heavy irony of that listing of women's central dependancy on 'Love'. The anger cools as the image of the phonecall incident develops into a direct statement of sexual politics. The ending is just as ironical, just as frustrated as that of *Aunt Jennifer's Tigers*, though one might argue that the 'poetry' becomes stark and 'unpoetic' as the poem works for its conclusion. *Translations* opens prosaically with a reference to another's poem. It develops an original set of images of its own, and also a dramatic situation within itself. It ends, however, with a prosaic statement of intent. The 'message' is underlined by the poet.

5 *Summarise my responses to the poem.*

These two poems share a common intention: they address the condition of women. However, in style, in their respective poetic strategies, they are quite distinct. *Aunt Jennifer's Tigers* instances one woman, trapped in a marriage which stunts her growth as an individual. She is manacled by her wedding ring and the conventional submission which that seems to represent. The deep irony is that she is in her very entrapment, her dependency on the 'womanly' task of embroidery, gazing at a screen which presents her with the very images of anger and freedom which she should emulate in her life. The poem predicts no such self-realisation and fulfilment for her, however. She is imagined in her coffin, her hands still 'terrified' into gestures of defeat, still 'ringed with ordeals she was masterd by'. And what a heavy weight that 'mastered' carries in the context of this poem.

Translations uses the strategy of addressing another person directly. The reader is allowed to listen in to this monologue. The effect is more direct, more confrontational than that of *Aunt Jennifer's Tigers*. There we are presented with a character almost as in a fiction. It is a skilfully crafted character study. *Translations* works by tracing the development of associations in the poet's (we assume the speaker's) mind. She is herself responding to language, especially to words which seem to have an elemental force; these words are basic to women's experience throughout the world and are therefore readily 'translatable' from language to language and from feelings to feelings. Part of the argument is that women are joined by their experiences across national and cultural borders, whereas Aunt Jennifer is located specifically in a Western, European or North American culture.

By its listing of various activities and its disjointing into short lines of the details of the narrative, the laborious tasks, *Translations* conveys the sense of a woman working her way through a series of thoughts to a conclusion. The argument finally rests on the political nature of women's entrapment, which is partly a consequence of their own inability to distinguish between 'Love' and 'love'. Of course, it now remains for each reader to give their own personal preference. Is *Translations* still too far from your expectations of *Poetry* to finally convince you that it is a considered and skilful poem? Or does it excite and provoke you as a piece of poetry which might actually shock readers into a more thoughtful consideration of gender roles and the position of women in various societies around the world? Is *Aunt Jennifer's Tigers*, for you, clearly a well-crafted poem, making its point with subtlety, developing an irony through its carefully chosen images? Is the wit and polish of this poem ultimately a far more effective means of protesting against the subjugation of women? A more stirring call to self-re-examination by both women and men?

What is *your* response? And how is that response altered if I now tell you, or if you had known from the first sight of these poems, that, in fact, *both* were written by Adrienne Rich, *Translations* some 21 years later than *Aunt Jennifer's Tigers*? And if I add that Adrienne Rich is an American (b.1929) and that she is now regarded as one of the leading feminist writers? She has stated that she no longer feels that she wants to write poetry of conventional 'quality', a poetry that has traditionally been praised by, and which has centred on 'male' values. Adrienne Rich was an active protester against the Vietnam war (a war she characterised as being a consequence of the domination of male needs and values) and she continues in her prose and poetry to be in the forefront of feminist thought.

'That's unfair!' you cry. 'How could I be expected to know those things?' And, of course, the whole point of a critical appraisal of an unseen text is that one should respond personally and directly to the text itself. There is, after all, a sense in which these two poems were written by different people, for Adrienne Rich, personally and artistically, had changed between the 1950s and the 1970s. How much more straightforward it would be if we could make lasting assumptions, firm generalisations regarding the authors and poets we have to study. The examination system with its reliance on themes and literary periods certainly encourages such approaches. But why should we assume that writers are more reliable, more consistent and better organised than we are ourselves?

What we can rely on, however, is the text before us as determined by the writer who has worked seriously and hard to bring a poem to a finished state. Ezra Pound said that 'A poem is never finished, only abandoned', and that carries the sense of writing as a careful, continuous reappraisal of the words. But Pound also, and I think unfortunately, implies there that a poem is somehow cast adrift, falling short of the ideal state for which it was intended. Poets publish work only when they are convinced that the poem is strong enough to float, at least as strong and effective as they can make it. That does not mean that you as a reader and critic have to admire or enjoy the poem. As long as you respect the intention of the writer, and you give the text sufficient time and attention, then your responses will be valid and your judgement, supported by specific references, will be worthy. Remember the five steps which I have outlined in this chapter:

1   What sort of writing is shaped in front of me?
2   Speak the poem to myself.
3   What patterns can I see in the poem?

4 Discuss any ambiguities or paradoxes in the poem.
5 Summarise my responses to the poem.

These should help you to reach that considered response. In my next chapter I want to show you how these five points are also involved in the process of writing a poem.

2

The Making of a Poem

IN 1984 a poem of mine won the National Poetry Competition. In this chapter I will show you how that poem came into being and the stages by which it developed into a publishable piece of writing. I will, then, be looking at a poem with you from *the other side of the text*, explaining how the poem's structure, pace, diction and imagery, emerge from my reworking of the text over a number of months and a series of drafts.

It is important to realise that the published poems, stories, novels or play-texts which you are asked to study on your courses are fixed, 'finished' texts only because the writer has worked them through to that state of completion. It is always interesting to view the notes and draft stages of a literary work, for we often find that the writer's own dilemmas in the composition may clarify those we experience as readers. It may come as a shock to some readers to realise that writers may not embark on a piece of writing knowing exactly what they are about or where the exercise may take them! This is not quite the case with my poem *The Death of Richard Beattie-Seaman in the Belgian Grand Prix, 1939*. That, if nothing else, is probably one of the longest titles you have come across! It is certainly the longest which I have ever used.

That poem has its starting point in a book which my wife gave me for Christmas in 1983. This was *The War Artists* by Meirion and Susie Harries, (Michael Joseph, London, 1983). I have been interested in the Great War since my days as a history student in school. As a sixth-former in the early 1960s I remember vividly the effect that a mammoth BBC documentary series had had on me. It was in 26 weekly parts, comprised entirely of contemporary films of the Great War and brought the horrific realities of the trenches home to me. I had encountered some of the poems of Wilfred Owen and Siegfried Sassoon already and was to read more thoroughly the poets of 1914-1918 as an English student at college.

THE DEATH OF RICHARD BEATTIE-SEAMAN
IN THE BELGIAN GRAND PRIX, 1939.

Trapped in the wreckage by his broken arm
he watched the flames flower from the front end.
So much pain—*Holy Jesus, let them get to me*—
so much pain he heard his screams like music
when he closed his eyes—the school organ at Rugby
Matins with light slanting down
hot and heady from the summer's high windows.
Pain—his trousers welded by flame to his legs.
His left hand tore off the clouded goggles—
rain falling like light into the heavy trees,
the track polished like a blade.
They would get to him, they were all coming
all running across the grass, he knew.

The fumes of a tuned Mercedes smelt like
boot polish and tear gas—coughing, his screams rising
high out of the cockpit—high
away to '38 *Die Nurburgring.*
He flew in with Clara
banking and turning the Wessex through a slow circle
over the scene—sunlight flashing off the line of cars,
people waving, hoardings and loudspeakers, swastikas
and the flags of nations lifted in the wind he stirred.
She held his arm tightly, her eyes were closed.
He felt strong like the stretched wing of a bird,
the course mapped out below him.
That day Lang and Von Brauchitsch and Caracciola
all dropped out and he did it—won
in the fourth Mercedes before a crowd of half a million
—the champagne cup, the wreath around his neck,
An Englishman the toast of Germany
The camera caught him giving a Hitlergruss.

Waving arms, shouts and faces, a mosaic
laid up to this moment—La Source—tight—the hairpin
the trees—tight—La Source—keeping up the pace
Belgium—La Source hairpin too tight.

With the fire dying, the pain dying
the voices blurred beneath the cool licks of rain.
To be laid under the cool sheets of rain.
A quiet with, just perceptible, engines roaring
as at the start of a great race.

The War Artists reminded me that the British had commissioned artists and sent them to draw and paint the fighting. This, perhaps odd, practice was introduced in the Great War, following the example of the Canadians. I was particularly struck by the work of an Irishman, William Orpen. (It is one of the quirks of twentieth-century British history that the Irish, too, died for the Empire in Flanders.) Orpen was a very famous and successful portrait painter in Edwardian England. He painted many of the notable political and 'society' figures and was an obvious choice when the war artists scheme was introduced. So it was that in 1917 Major Orpen went to Flanders, to war in style – chauffeur-driven in one of his Rolls Royces, with a batman and a business manager. I was struck by the way in which Orpen responded to the horrors of the war, after his high life and subject matter back in London.

William Orpen also produced a number of portraits of a very beautiful woman. She was his lover and he continued his affair with her for some years after the war. I discovered that Orpen had fabricated an elaborate story to explain these paintings to his masters back at the War Office. The story became a *cause célèbre* and Orpen had to use all his influence with notable pre-war portrait subjects in order to maintain his position as an official war artist. I wrote a poem which dramatically reconstructed some of these facts, *William Orpen and Yvonne Aubicq in the Rue Dannon*. I had also written a poem at this time from the point of view of two soldiers in the trenches and was working on another about the experiences of a young English woman caught up in the war on the Russian front, where she became a Red Cross nurse.

Researching Orpen's story further by reading his biography (*Mirror to an Age*, by Bruce Arnold) I discovered that when his affair with Yvonne finally ended he presented her with a Rolls Royce as a parting gift, with his chauffeur, Frederick Grover Williams as her driver. Well, she married him shortly afterwards and Grover Williams became a racing driver, and quite a successful one, winning the Monaco Grand Prix in 1929 and settling in France to race up until the Second World War. It was in reading about the immensely popular motor-racing world of the 1930s that I came across the story of Richard Beattie-Seaman.

Perhaps I should point out that I have absolutely no interest in this sport. What attracted me to further reading was the deep irony of Seaman's position. It was his tragedy to have been caught up by his sporting enthusiasm in a bizarre episode of history. A monied Englishman, with a public school education, young, handsome, a qualified pilot who died in the flames of a cockpit in Belgium in 1939. Of course, that sounds like the climax of a dozen black and white war films of the 1940s and 1950s, doesn't it? The fact that the cockpit was that of a racing car; that the car was a Mercedes Benz, and that Mercedes were a German firm very much under the control of the Nazis, these facts presented an irony which I felt I could examine further through a poem. Then I came across these photographs (see page 33).

I have always reacted to photographs and have produced a number of poems from published and family prints. It seems that many poets glean ideas from such sources. In this case, that juxtaposition of Richard Beattie-Seaman and the failed Austrian painter, Hitler himself, was the final ingredient which determined my commitment to the poem. That Englishman was close enough to have swung a starting-handle at Hitler and by so doing have changed the course of history. Later that year he was, instead, to win the German Grand Prix for Mercedes and, albeit with embarrassment and reluctance, to raise his arm on the victory rostrum in a Nazi salute.

Those photographs were the catalyst which compelled me on to the page. I *had* to write down, in some order, the range of fascinating details which had come from my reading of several chapters about motor racing in the thirties. The first stage of the poem was, then, a scribbled attempt to compose notes. Still, as you may see, the notes are, from the beginning, consciously formed as poem-lines (see page 34).

Where and when possible I try to write first attempts of poems on a single sheet of paper. I feel secure if I can work within the *frame* of a single page. That way I can hold the shape and work on the structure of the potential poem. It wasn't possible in this instance: perhaps I was too tentative about the possibility of working this mass of information into a poem; I mean 'working' in the sense that a potter works clay into a finished pot. Perhaps I was simply careless. In any case, the page had to be turned over and the scribbling continued (see page 35).

At first sight, what we appear to have in this first draft is little more than a scribbled, jumbled set of events and impressions. But I remember feeling that there were already lines and groups of lines which were sufficiently interesting and

TWILIGHT OF THE GODS
*Above: The Mercedes team of 1938. Left to right are: von
Brauchitsch, team manager Neubauer, Richard Seaman, Hermann
Lang and Rudolf Caracciola. Below: Visitors to Mercedes. Only
Hitler seemed to find the noise deafening.*

Draft 1

The death of Richard Beattie-Seaman.

Seaman flew into Nürburgring
~~they flew in~~ He flew in with her.
He ~~clanked~~ing and turning in a slow circle
over the scene – sunlight flashing off the lines of cars
~~reflecting~~ moving hoardings + ~~many~~ trees + the nations' flags
(loudspeakers)
taut in the wind he stirred.
The ~~Nürburgring~~ course laid out like a map
below him

~~Seaman~~ On the 22nd lap in the Belgian in '39
he spun out of a hairpin called La Source
and ~~skidded~~ into a tree

~~trapped~~ by his broken arm in the wreckage
he watched the flames flower from the front-end.
So much pain – they would get to him –
so much pain ~~his scream~~ he heard his screams like music
as the organ at Rugby chapel. – ~~mass~~ of Sunday service
~~then~~ with light ~~slanting~~ down on them
from the windows – his ~~legs~~ welded by heat
                    trousers
to ~~of~~ the legs –
His left hand tore off the goggles' oil-clouds
Rain falling, the trees heavy with it, rain-polished
the track.

the fire dead, the pain dead, & then
~~the~~ cool rain, voices, / the cool sheets. A quiet
with, just perceptible, engines roaring
as at the start of a great race.

~~Dick flew into~~
Dick flew his plane in to the German in '38

they would get to him — Dr Glaeser
truly Caracciola — skidding out of it after five
would be flicked in the pits. — they were coming
the fumes of the Mercedes smelt like boot polish mixed
with tear gas.
~~the~~ coughing, screaming high out of the cockpit
high, away back to '38 Nürburgring

                    IN SORT,

I know that day lung & Von Brauchitsch, & Caracciola
all fell out & he did it. ~~✷~~ War in the
Mercedes before 350,000 people
the ~~death~~ the art, the title, the wealth
from Kraftfahrer Hehnlein
"An Englishman — the toast of Germany.

had some qualities of tension, drama, even some poetic tricks of alliteration and assonance, to justify further commitment to the poem. Turning the page back over, however, to see what I had written I surveyed a bit of a shambles. The first scene is set at Nurburgring, the famous German Grand Prix circuit, but my title, and intention is clearly underlined. It is the *death* of Seaman which is the compelling fact of the story. Also, it is a *story* which I feel that I'm engaged on in this piece of writing. That being the case, what is the most effective starting point? I sensed very quickly that the story, the poem, should open at the point of Seaman's death, and not at Nurburgring the previous year. The story was going to be told achronologically, that is not in the order in which the historical events actually happened.

My opening lines of handwriting are, though, still of importance, not just because of the scene and the date, but because I felt I must write from the very beginning from *Seaman's point of view*. That fact is the single most important controlling force in this poem. Though I never consciously chose to experience the story as Seaman – that must, I suppose, have been the effect of the story upon me – I empathised with the man. I was certainly excited by the eleventh and twelfth lines of scribble –

> Trapped by his broken arm in the wreckage
> he watched the flames flower from the front-end.

Surely, I felt, the horror of that imprisonment in the burning car would 'grab' readers and impel them too into the details of this man's story?

In fact, the following eleven lines, down to 'great race', contain the complete structure of the final poem, and, though I could not have known it at this early stage, I must have sensed it, because I then begin and immediately abandon a return to my opening, 'Dick flew into . . . Dick flew his plane into the German in '38', and just down the page I strongly urge myself to 'INSERT' other details in some way into or after the initial drama of the crash. There is, though, already too much going on in my brain and the sooner I get things down on to paper, the better. Perhaps more than some other, more organised poets, I need to move quite quickly on to the typewriter (or, more recently, the word-processor). My handwriting is pretty poor and, practising what I preach, I *see* poems in lines primarily, that is as shaped

writing. It is the act of committing the handwritten draft to the
typewriter that begins, quickly, to clarify many of the confusions
regarding length, pace and structure in this poem. As you may
now see (page 38).

That dramatic first line is leading the first section of the poem
into a unity which is encouraging. I want to establish Seaman's
entrapment, and the loss of consciousness as a consequence
of the intensity of the pain he's experiencing. I am weaving
together the present and the distant past, his boyhood, coming
back to the present with the reference to the team manager, Dr
Glaeser, and the others, all of them surely rushing to his aid. At
this stage, I am still anxious to name names, to inform readers
of the context of the race and the Mercedes team, as well as to
characterise Beattie-Seaman and to point out the treacherous
conditions that day. The middle section of the handwritten, first
draft has definitely become the opening of the poem.

That simile, in line 15, comparing the smell of the exhaust
fumes to tear gas and boot polish, was actually made by a contemporary British driver in one of the source books I had used.
I say 'had used' because from this point I did not refer again to
those books on motor racing. I felt that I had enough information.
Perhaps too many details are making claims for inclusion in the
poem at this point? The smell of the car, exaggerated by the fire, is
the sensory trigger for Seaman. Coughing and screaming, he will
again escape the horror of the present circumstances by drawing
on better times from his memory. I felt, and still feel, that this is
a perfectly credible, even predictable detail. The body has a sort
of cut-out mechanism when challenged by extreme pain.

The gap after 'Nurburgring '38' is the clearest indication that
this draft is continuing to grapple with the problem of pace and
narrative direction, the problem which made the first draft such
a confusion of intentions. The key to the poem's success will be
held in that problem: I want the poem to 'sandwich' the past in
between a narrative in the present tense. That present tense will,
necessarily, be in real time no more than a minute or two as the
crippled driver succumbs to the heat, smoke and pain. *Speaking
the poem to myself* (you try this) it seems that the events are already
detailed and that the poem has substance, though the real time of
the story is brief. I want to build on that tension of pace, spacing
out the consequences of the crash, making the film play in slow

Draft 2

The Death of Richard Beattie-Seaman

Trapped· by his broken arm in the wrechage
he watched the flames flower from the front end.
So much páin - they would get to him -
so much pain he heard his screams like music
~~thexorganxatxRMERYxchapeixxxx~~
summer   - the chapel organ at Rugby (when he closed his eyes)
Sunday service with light slanting down on them
from the high windows (hot and heady)-/his trousers
wáăded by the flames to his legs -
his left hand tore off the goggles' oilyclouds -
rain falling, the trees heavy with it.
Rain-polished the track.
They would get to him - Dr Gaeser,
the crew,   Rudy Caracciola skidding out of it after five
would be back at the pits -/they were coming *all*   *he knew   long & leant in the lights*

The fumes of the Mercedes smelt like boot polish
with tear gas
- coughing, screaming high out of the cockpit
high - away back to Nurburgring '38.

He flew in with her
banking and turning a slow circle
over the scene - sunlight flashing off the line of cars,   *tight*
people waving, hoardings and loudspeakers, swaztikas *She tells this on*
and the nations' flags taut in the wind he stirred.   *he felt loop was closed.*
The course laid out like a map beneath him
a crowd of ½ a million   and how that day Lang and Von Brauchitsch and Caracciola   *he felt they*
all/out and he did it. Won in the Mercedes, last Mercedes *strong*
before 350,000 people. - the cup, the title, the wreath   *like a bird*
from Korpsfuhrer Hehnlein:
An Englishman the toast of Germany

keep of the pace
Now Belgium, the hairpin - tight - la Source-   *the hi/ forme fontain*
the trees - tight - la Source- tight -   *too tight*

now the fire dead, the pain dead and then
the cool rain - voices - the cool sheets -
A quiet with, just perceptible, ebgines roaring
as at the start of a great race.

motion, as it were. That ploy also has the effect of contrasting actual time and narrative pace, encouraged by the irony of a race at high speed suddenly brought to a halt. A visual blur at racing speed brought down to a blurring of perceptions through trauma and the escape into memory. All those decisions are to do with my first critical step – *What patterns can I see in the poem?*

Perhaps at this stage I have made two very fundamental decisions: first, this material is not going to be susceptible to a poetic realisation through the traditional means of regular metre and standard verses; second, the delivery of the story as a three-part poem – present tense/ memory/ present again – will serve to heighten and maintain the reader's interest. At this stage, too, the four sections of the poem are unsatisfactory. I have already mentioned that awkward transitional gap after 'Nurburgring '38', but there is also that very disjointed final six-line section which is trying to provide more information about the race track whilst preparing for the last, and strangely peaceful moments of Richard Beattie-Seaman's life. I seem to be content with the images of coolness and interrupted quiet, but still to be unsure about that staccato listing, almost chanting, of the Belgian details.

The other changes concern the third section. I imagine Beattie-Seaman flying into the German Grand Prix with a woman. Now, I had no information concerning this man's private life, and so, I suppose, was interpolating a facet of his character and life style for which I had no historical justification. However, I would want to argue that in placing a woman *on his arm* I am, at least, not stretching one's credulity. A young, handsome racing driver would, in all probability, attract the attentions of many women. The artistic, *factional*, if not fictional point which I am making is that Richard Beattie-Seaman at the time of the German Grand Prix in 1938 must have felt secure, successful, happy. I wanted to present him at the height of his powers, at some climax of his short life, flying his own plane into that race, the challenge of the course mapped out below him and perhaps the sense of a possible victory that day.

The only other change is a cosmetic one: '350,000', in line 29, is, in fact, the size of the crowd at that race, but my use of figures and the documentary effect of precisely noting the volume of people adds but another detail to a poem which has details and names enough. The scanning of that line with '350,000' is clumsy and overlong, and so, I felt, had to be changed. This is a good example of the way in which writers may seriously test their work by sounding out the words.

Having said that, the next draft would seem to compound such details in its new title (see page 41).

This becomes the final version of the title because I felt that the poem was making considerable demands on the reader and that I should, from the outset, establish the particular time and place of the poem. Having a title of such length and particularity also has the effect of immediately persuading the reader that this piece of writing is rooted in actuality. These events took place in history. Of course, that is true of the man Richard Beattie-Seaman and his racing career and his death. But the title also helps to persuade the reader that Seaman's experiences as I have imagined them are valid, that this is the way it would actually have happened.

More importantly, this third draft commits the poem to its four final section lengths. The long second section is unified by the joining of 'The fumes . . . ' to 'He flew in . . . ', because I am anxious to make that rather difficult transition of place and time, from Belgium in 1939 to Germany in 1938, as clear and natural as it can be for the reader. I am concentrating on this part of the poem almost exclusively in this draft. That is a practical procedure for me, and for other poets, I gather. One needs to concentrate on specific problems in turn once the overall sense of the poem is recorded. By focusing on one verse or section, one sentence, one line, even one image or word, you bring your whole energy to bear on the problem. As each of these problems is addressed in turn, the poem should grow stronger and stronger.

To that end I am in the process of switching ''38' and 'Nurburgring', in line 19, so that the date comes first to emphasise the flashback nature of the mind's working, triggered by the pain. As Richard Beattie-Seaman's screams rise, in a sense escape the pain of the present, so his mind substitutes the triumph of the previous year for the horror of the crash. Even though this device attracts me I can see that it could still prove to be confusing for the reader. As this point of the poem acts as a sort of fulcrum on which I balance the poem, it is clear that I shall have to put in further work to clarify and secure the intention. It is to this end that I develop a better sense of the relationship with Clara. Clara? Yes, the 'she' of the earlier drafts has become 'Clara'. I feel that it is nearly always more effective, more evocative to name people (to name places, flowers, machines and to use

Draft 3

The Deathof Richard Beattie-Seaman
in the Belgian Grand Prix,1939.

Trapped in the wreckage by his broken arm
he watched the flames flower from the front end.
So much pain - they would get to him -
so much pain he heard his screams like music
when he closed his eyes - the chapel organ at Rugby
Sunday service with light slanting down on them
hot and heady from the summer's high windows -
pain - his trousers welded by flame to his legs -
his left hand tore off the goggles' oil-clouds-
rain falling,the trees heavy with it.
The track rain-polished.
They would get to him - Dr Glaesery the crew.
Rudy Caracciola losing it at a bend in the fifth
would be back at the pits -they were all coming
he knew.

The fumes of a tuned Mercedes smelt like
boot polish and tear gas - coughing,screaming
high put of the cockpit - high   *look to '38 Die Nurburging*
away back to Nurburgring '38   *any*
- he flew in withber *Clara Vesey/Mayr*
banking and turning the Avro through a slow circles
over the scene sunlight flashing off the line of cars,
people waving,hoardings and loudspeakers, swastikas
and the nations' flags taut in the wind he stirred.
She held his arm tightly, her eyes were closed.
He felt strong - the stretched wing of a bird,
the course laid out like a map below him.
And how that day Lang and Von Brauchitsch and Caracciola
all dropped out and he did it - won
     in the last Mercedes before acrowd of half a million
- the cup,the title,the wreath   *and his neck*
from Korpsfuhrer Hehnlein:
An Englishman the boast of Germany

Shouts, faces, waving arms, a mosaic -
now Belgium,the hairpin - tight - La Soyrce -
the trees - tight - La Source - keeping up the pace
- the La Source hairpin too tight.

Now the fire dead, the pain dead and then
the cool licks of rain -voices -tongues
the cool sheets of rain.
A quiet with, just perceptible, engines roaring
as at the start of a great race.

brand names for specific effects). What was I to call Richard Beattie-Seaman's companion? I certainly did not wish to opt for too obviously a Germanic name – Eva, Helga or such. I speak and understand no German, but, luckily, teach at a college which does have a languages department. I consulted a colleague and wondered whether 'Clara' might not be acceptable. He said that it was, and I was pleased to be able to use a name at once convincingly Germanic and having Lawrentian echoes.

In the following line 21, I name the aeroplane which he flies: 'Avro' sounded convincingly 1930s to my ear, but on checking through a book of civil aircraft of the period at my public library I found a number of other possibilities. From these I chose 'Wessex', (dismissing 'Dragon' in the process). If I confess that, in fact, the Wessex was an aircraft of medium passenger-carrying proportions, and that therefore Seaman was almost certainly *not* using such a plane for his private travel, what might you conclude? Whether you know that or not, it should be noted that whenever a writer uses such a specific detail, a manu-facturer's name or model number, they are signalling something. There is quite often a social or personal significance attached to such details. Here, 'Wessex' is appropriate artistically, because it is so English. Wessex was one of the ancient kingdoms of Britain and was brought effectively back into the consciousness of this century by Thomas Hardy in his novels, all of which were set in the West Country he defined as Wessex.

The only other point to note from this section in Draft 3 is that the victory wreath is now 'around his neck'. I think that deepens the irony of the ceremony, making a firmer play on 'wreath' and making it become a portent of the fate which awaits Seaman. I am still playing off that 'wreath' against the irony of the Nazis' motor-racing organiser's name in the line which follows. 'Korpsfuhrer' has a nightmarish connotation for non-German speakers, doesn't it?

Although you will be unable to perceive this on the draft as presented in this book, I should point out that the line

An Englishman the toast of Germany

is typed at this stage in blue. This is a direct quote from one of my sources of an English newspaper headline after the race, and I wish to distinguish it as such. However, the significance of the blue ribbon will be dealt with further in the next draft (see p. 44).

In the second line of that second section 'coughing, screaming' has become 'coughing, his screams rising . . . '. I felt that this emphasised the sense of escape; the conception of Seaman himself escaping from the burning car, lifted away by his own screams of pain. Other amendments to this section attempt to clarify the scene – ' the flags of nations lifted'; then 'the course mapped out; the 'fourth Mercedes', rather than the 'last Mercedes', which is confusing as a reference to the winning car; 'the *champagne* cup' enhances the importance of the win and I am prepared to lose the words 'the title' as a consequence from a line which is now too long. It is the scribbled line, however, which encloses the flashback part of the section and the instruction 'Blue, / italics' which is the surest indication that this point of the poem is still causing considerable concern. I am worried whether I shall lose my reader at this vital part of the narrative and the poem.

In the first section I decide to change 'on them' in line 6 to focus on Seaman's school perceptions alone. The positioning of 'Pain' in line 7 will continue to be varied in the next draft. I am also dissatisfied with the ending of the first section. The description of the Mercedes crew and their manager, Dr Glaeser, and what their reaction is to the crash, these things are troubling me. Poets, and of course novelists, often have problems in the very fact that they need to transport characters from one place to another. One wants to focus on the central character, but he or she is dependant on others, they need to relate to other characters. It is obvious that when a sportsperson achieves a great victory that there is a range of people in support of that achievement, but it is not necessary for the supporter, fan or, in this case, reader, to be aware of those background people. Again, I am bowing under the weight of too much researched information regarding the Belgian Grand Prix.

In the two short sections which conclude the poem I am working in this draft to substantiate the first-person perspective of Richard Beattie-Seaman. I am trying to intensify the staccato effect of the final flickering consciousness in the third section by further disjointing the syntax of the impressionistic 'mosaic' which leads like some mosaic floor, it seems inevitably, up to this moment. To that same end, I change the tense of the final five lines, attempting to underline the return of the poem to its

Draft 4

The death of Richard Beattie-Seaman
in the Belgian Grand Prix,1939.

Trapped in the wreckage by his broken arm
he watched the flames flower from the front end.
So much pain - they would get to him -
so much pain he heard his screams like music
when he closed his eyes - the school organ at Rugby
Sunday service with light slanting down on them ~~~ *a Pain —*
hot and heady from the summer's high windows - *a Pain —*
(pain) - his trousers welded by flame to his legs.
His left hand tore off the goggles' oil-clouds
rain falling, the trees heavy with it,
the track rain-polished.
They would get to him - Dr.Gläeser, the crew,
Rudy Caracciola losing it at a bend in the fifth
would be back at the pits - they wereall coming
he knew.

all running across the grass

The fumes of a tuned Mercedes smelt like
boot polish and tear gas - coughing, screaming *roaring*
high out of the cockpit - high
away back to '38 Nurburgring.
He flew in with Clara
banking and turning the Wessex through a slow circle
over the scene - sunlight flashing off the line of cars,
people waving,hoardings,and loudspeakers, swastikas
and the nations' flags that in the wind he stirred.
She held his arm tightly, her eyes were closed.
He felt strong as the stretched wing of a bird,
the course laid out like a map below him.
That day Lang and Von Brauchitsch and Caracciola
all dropped out and he did it - won
in the last Mercedes before a crowd of half a million
- the cup, the title, the wreath around his neck
the speech from Korpsfuhrer Hehnlein :
An Englishman the toast of Germany.

flags of nations   *the tab*   *champagne*

Shouts, faces, waving arms, a mosaic -
now Belgium,the hairpin - tight - La Source -
the trees, tight - La Source - keeping up the pace
- the La Source hairpin too tight.

up to this moment   *Belgium*   *blue land*   *up to then - tight - the hairpin la Source*

With   *dying*   *dying*   *come*
Now the fire dead, the pain dead and then
the cool licks of rain - voices -tongues *the blurred voices behind rain*
the cool sheets of rain.
A quiet with, just perceptible,engines roaring
as at the start of a great race.

the

With the fire dying, the pain dying,
the voices blurred and beneath the cool licks of rain.
To be laid under the cool sheets of rain
A quiet with - - - - - - race

present and its beginning. 'The blurred voices' and 'the cool licks of rain' create, I hope, a tantalisingly imprecise, yet sensual effect. Incidentally, poets and other writers have words which reappear again and again in their work. It's as if they were craving the taste of these words. 'Blur' is one of mine and I can justify its use here because it has exactly the right combination of effects in its onomatopoeia and its sense of rendering pictures and perceptions imprecise.

'Blur' holds another suggestion, though. My poem hinges on my persuading readers that they should empathise with Richard Beattie-Seaman. They should move from a cinema-audience, voyeur's experience of the events in the poem to commit themselves to a closer affinity with the central character. The shift in time which happens in the second section is vital in that it seeks to relieve the horrible intensity of the opening scene (for both Seaman and the reader), and because I want Seaman to be fixed in the specific historical context of a Europe dominated by Nazi ambition and aggression. At the same time I want to keep the effect of that slipping out of the present to the past, from immediate perception into memory. But how can I achieve that? Should I simply indent the whole of the second section, so that it shapes up differently on the page? Certainly, the typography should signify that intention. Would an asterik do? The blue type is impractical both for printing and xeroxing, so that cannot be a long-term solution. In any case, I don't really want the whole of that section to be highlighted. What I really want is to shift time more subtly, in the middle of a line, in the same way that Richard Beattie-Seaman's mind would have escaped the painful present for the sweet memory of victory.

The next draft, Draft 5, indicates how, quite by chance, the problem was solved for me (see page 46).

Only by being able to change the basic appearance of the print in the second section am I able to signify the change from 1939 back to 1938. And that facility was, through sheer luck afforded me by the fact that in the Autumn Term of 1984 my college changed its office practice from electric typewriters to word-processors. I inherited a very serviceable IBM 'golf ball' machine. This enabled me to shift into italic print in the middle of a line or sentence simply by inserting a 'golf ball' with a different print style.

The pertinent point here for you, as reader and critic, is that

Draft 5   Th*e* Death of Richard Beattie-Seaman
in the Belgian Grand Prix,1939

— Holy Jesus, let them get to me — — Italis

Trapped in the wreckage by his broken arm
he watched the flames flower from the front end.
So much pain - ~~they would get to him -~~
so much pain he heard his screams like music
when he closed his eyes - the school organ at Rugby
~~Sunday service~~ with light slanting down
hot and heady from the summer's high windows. (Pain)
- pain - - his trousers welded by flame to his legs.
His left hand tore off the goggles' oil-clouds -
rain falling, the trees heavy with it,
the track rain-polished.
They would get to him - Dr. Glaeser, the crew,
Rudy Caracciola losing it at a bend in the fifth
would be back at the pits - they were all coming
all running across the grass, he knew.

The fumes of a tuned .Mercedes smelt like
boot polish and tear gas - coughing, his screams rising
high out of the cockpit - high
away back to '38 *Die Nurburgring*.
He flew in with Clara   *moth*
banking and turning the Wessex through a slow circle
over the scene - sunlight flashing off the line of cars,
people waving, hoardings and loudspeakers, swastikas
and the flags of nations lifted in the wind he stirred.
She held his arm tightly, her eyes were closed.
~~Hh~~ felt strong like the stretched wing of a bird,
the course mapped out below him.
That day Lng and Von Brauchitsch and Carraciola
all dropped out and he did it - won
in the fourth Mercedes before a crowd of half a million
- the champagne cup, the wreath around his neck,
~~*the speech from Korpsfuhrer Hehnlein*~~
An *E*nglishman the toast of ~~Germany~~

Waving arms, shouts, faces, a mosaic
laid up to this moment - La source - tight-the hairpin
the trees-tight La Source- Keeping up the pace
(Belgium) the La Source hairpin too tight.

With the fire dying, the pain dying
the voices blurred beneath the cool licks of rain.
To be laid under the cool sheets of rain.
A quiet with, just perceptible, engines roaring
as at the start of a great race.

any variation in the physical appearance of a text, in its spacing, its shaping on the page, and in its print format –

> *italic*
> **bold**
> or UPPER CASE

– is signifying or modifying the author's intention as surely as their choice of words, their diction or the order of those words – their syntax. We saw how important William Carlos Williams' lack of punctuation and use of the capital letter was in 'This is just to say' and in Adrienne Rich's *Translations*. Physical appearance of the text will be absolutely central to the working practice, the aesthetics of modern and contemporary poets such as Apollinaire, Carl Sandburg, the 'Black Mountain' poets of America, the 'Liverpool Poets', the 'Beat poet' Ferlinghetti and the Scot Edwin Morgan.

I would also like to make the point that writers have particular working practices or working circumstances which facilitate their writing. I have been told by Alan Sillitoe that he writes his novels standing up, with a fountain pen. Barry Hines, the author of *A Kestrel for a Knave*, writes in long-hand, a pile of blank sheets on the desk to his right slowly becoming a pile of manuscript sheets to his left as he pursues his narrative. Alan Sillitoe reworks each novel or story six or seven times. He then types the work speedily, (having been taught to type during his time as a clerk in the RAF). Barry Hines lifts the finished left-hand pile to his right once more and repeats the procedure a second time before dispatching the manuscript to be typed. Beryl Bainbridge works most of her paragraphs over and over, almost as if each were a poem, polished and self-contained. Many writers of fiction now work with word-processors, and poets too seem to be able to make more flexible demands of their 'hardware' as Dylan Thomas did with his bus-tickets and beer-mats. I am sure that my acquisition of the IBM typewriter significantly changed the style, if not the concerns, of my poetry from 1984 to the point at which I bought an Amstrad word-processor in 1987. It is, of course, not necessary for readers to be aware of such practices. However, the reader must be prepared to respond to the exactitude of the finished text, for all serious writers, whatever the circumstances of their craft, are concerned to determine absolutely the final version of the text which they intend.

Draft 5 of my poem may look no tidier than the other typed versions, but it is the occasion for most of the major problems to be solved. In the first section I decide to give Richard Beattie-Seaman a voice. The screams he utters in the middle of the poem are so vital to the organisation of the narrative that I felt it would strengthen that moment to hear the trapped driver calling for deliverance. I had been repositioning that third, insistent 'pain' in the previous draft, partly to add to the near-rhyming of 'arm' and 'Him'. My insertion of 'Holy Jesus, let them get to me – ' in line 3, in any case, sets up another rhyme with 'Rugby' and I welcome that. Though this poem does not organise itself by means of a rhyming pattern, I do want to set up a poetic tension against the onward thrust of the narrative. I am concerned to *foreground* language as any poet would, whilst preserving the impulse, the pace of a fascinating story. I have been, you may remember, concerned from the very first, scribbled draft of this text to present the story (and my examination of the character and historical circumstances of that story) by means of discernible lines of poetry. One of the ways in which I can strengthen the poetic qualities of the text is to suggest or achieve rhyme, both at the end of some lines and internally between other lines. For example, 'rising', 'Nurburgring' and 'Hehnlein'; and 'Clara', 'cars' and 'Swastikas' all from the second section. Although it is no sonnet, *The Death of Richard Beattie-Seaman in the Belgian Grand Prix 1939* is proclaiming itself unmistakably to be a poem in its structure and its effects of language. Faced with the task of responding critically to such a text, you would do well to use that tension between the poetic/metaphorical qualities and the prosaic/narrative qualities of the poem. That is the point at which two of our basic critical approaches meet – *What patterns can I see in the poem?* and *Discuss any ambiguities or paradoxes in the poem.* I shall return to summarise responses to both those issues at the end of this chapter. For the moment, let us return to the final emendations to the poem in Draft 5.

Still in the second section: I am worrying (at this distance it seems unduly) over Seaman's aeroplane. Can I really get away with 'Wessex'? Wouldn't 'Moth' be more accurate? Further down, and of more importance, I finally exclude Korpsfuhrer Hehnlein from the poem. By adding a new closing line, line 33, to that section I can retain the sense of the racing team's involvement with the Nazis; further, the detail describing Beattie-Seaman's raised arm in the infamous Nazi fashion, the 'Hitlergruss' or Hitler salute, deepens the irony of the Englishman's compromise. This is the arm, is it not, which we already know will break and trap him in the flames a year later?

The third section shows relatively minor adjustments to my intended 'mosaic' effect. In particular I'm wondering whether I need to move 'Belgium', (line 37), to earlier in the section, so that I may underline the switch back to the present of the poem. I finally decide that the move is not necessary because now, with the insertion of 'The cameras caught him giving a Hitlergruss', the last line of the previous section is also in italics, and the typography is a sufficiently clear indication of the time change.

Going back to the first section, we can see another relatively minor change in that 'Sunday service' becomes 'Matins' in line 6. I was sorry to lose the rather restful alliteration of those 's' sounds, which contrasted so well with the anguished screams of the trapped racing driver. However, I finally decided that 'Sunday service' sounded too much like a Welsh chapel worship and that 'Matins' had the effect of underlining the essentially English, public school background of the man. Incidentally, yes, I did realise that 'high windows' was the title of Philip Larkin's last collection of poems. It's what I wanted to say about the chapel and I was prepared to risk the distraction of such a literary red herring.

Draft 6 essentially completes the fine tuning of that first section, whilst confirming those changes made to the other parts of the poem in the previous draft (see p. 50).

As you may see, the important changes in this draft are confined to those lines from line 9 to the end of the first section. Lines 9, 10 and 11 have had a clipped, abrupt effect up to this point. They create the feeling that Seaman's perceptions are discrete, moving from one fact to the next. I had come to think that I wanted the impression of a slowing down, following the frantic tearing off of the goggles. The new lines substantially slow down the whole movement and series of perceptions. I found, in any case, that 'His left hand tore off the goggles' oil-clouds – ' was difficult to say. I had discovered this and other problems of phrasing after including the poem in a public poetry reading. If

Draft 6

The Death of Richard Beattie-Seaman
in the Belgian Grand Prix, 1939

Trapped in the wreckage by his broken arm
he watched the flames flower from the front end.
So much pain -*Holy Jesus,let them get to me* -
so much pain he heard his screams like music
when he closed his eyes - the school organ at Rugby
Matins with the light slanting down
hot and heady from the summer's high windows.
Pain - his trousers welded by flame to his legs.   *louded goggles*
His left hand tore off the goggles' oil-clouds -
rain falling, the trees heavy with the   *long trees*
the track rain-polished, *like a blade*
They would get to him,- Dr Glaeser, the crew,   *cut for*
Rudy Carraciola losing is at a bend in the fifth   *completion.*
would be back at the pits - they were all coming
all running across the grass, he knew.

The fumes of a tuned Mercedes smelt like
boot polish and tear gas - coughing, his screams rising
high out of the cockpit - high
away back to '38 *Die Nurburgring.*
He flew in with Clara
banking and turning the Wessex through a slow circle
over the scene - sunlight flashing oof the line of cars,
people waving, hoardings and loudspeakers,swastikas
and the flags of nations lifted in the wind he stirred.
She held his arm tightly, her eyes were closed.
He felt strong like the stretched wing of a bird,
the course mapped out below him.
That day long *and Von Brauchitsch and Cracciola*
all dropped out and he did it - won
in the fourth Mercedes before a crowd of half a million
- the champagne cup, the wreath around his neck,
An Englishman the toast of Germany
The cameras caught him giving a Hitlergruss.

Waving arms, shouts and faces, a mosaic
laid up to this moment - La Source - tight- the hairpin
the trees - tight - La Source - keeping up the pace
Belgium - La Source hairpin too tight.

Withe the fire dying, the pain dying
the voices blurred beneath the cool licks of rain.
To be laid under the cool sheets of rain.
A quiet with, just perceptible, engines roaring
as at the start of a great race.

sounding the poem is a great help in determining meaning and
the precise effect of language, then the business of reading, or
performing, such a poem-in-progress in front of an audience who
have no copy of the text is especially illuminating for the poet –
in almost equal measure to the degree of mystification evident
in the audience!

In line 12, Dr Glaeser goes the way of Korpsfuhrer Hehnlein.
And Rudy Caracciola, who is credited as a colleague of Richard
Beattie-Seaman's later in the poem, is removed. I realised
that Caracciola's fate, simply that of losing the race through
mechanical problems, was a detail of little importance to the
central character's experiences in this poem. Striking out these
lines ensures that the first section is focused exclusively on
Seaman. And that strengthens the overall structure of the poem:
we begin with Seaman and his immediate view of the world from
that burning car; we go back in time through his memory and
discover the wider context of his involvement with racing and,
specifically, Mercedes; the poem returns us to the present, to
Richard Beattie-Seaman's now quite confused perceptions of his
surroundings, and finally to the salving relief of the rain, the
dying of the voices and the intimation of other engines firing
into action.

If the poem works, then it is because the potentially confusing
range of historical information and the shifting perspective of
character perceptions are finally fused in that last section. For the
poem to work it must have satisfied the same five considerations
which I have proposed as useful critical approaches for readers
and students.

1   *What sort of writing is shaped in front of me?*

It was clear from the very first scribbled draft that the material,
the story which I had stumbled across, and then worked for,
was unlikely to be expressed through a poem which organised
itself by the traditional means of rhyme and rhythm. I did not
feel that the nature of the material was such that a *Ballad of
Richard Beattie-Seaman* would be appropriate. The presentation of
the driver's experiences and the establishment of the situation
as a sporting/political/historical complex could not be effectively
achieved in regular verses of four, five or six lines. However, it was
just as clear to me that a poem was the only way for *me* to explore

and recreate these historical events. I am no novelist, and the sort of complexity of experiences and issues which had drawn me to the story of Richard Beattie-Seaman seemed to demand either a full-length biographical treatment – a film or novel – or a poetic cross section of that complex of events and experiences that would reveal the essential issues which I felt the story to contain, whilst not engaging in a conventional mimetic way with those events and experiences.

I was aware that the poem, nevertheless, did have to pattern itself in a way which would firstly drawn the reader into an empathy with Richard Beattie-Seaman and then exhibit the point of the story, the irony of the situation. The four sections of the finished piece achieve this as well as I am able. The opening is sufficiently dramatic and shocking to grip the reader; the idea of the mind escaping to another time is introduced early on and the first section mirrors the overall structure of the poem by returning at its end to the present and the relief of the driver's suffering.

The second section appears to alter the pace and focus of the poem with its apparently minor detail of 'The fumes of a tuned Mercedes', but there is a connection both in the way in which Seaman's mind is actively detaching itself from the pain of the present and in the echo of 'knew' from 'all running across the grass, he knew', and 'fumes' and 'tuned'.

This section manages, after much anguish and technical fiddling, to engineer that 'escape' in the mind of Richard Beattie-Seaman. The change of typeface in the fourth line of the section exemplifies that shift of tense and reality. The final line of the section shows Seaman giving a 'Hitlergruss' and this becomes transformed into the 'Waving arms' of the crowd at the Belgian Grand Prix the following year at the beginning of the third section. Occasionally at public readings, particularly in front of larger audiences, I will gesture a rather half-hearted 'Hitlergruss' at the end of that second section and turn the gesture into a wave as I move onto the third section. In truth, I find that even the suggestion of that Nazi salute invokes a strange and repulsive feeling in both the audience and myself.

I certainly pause between the third and final sections, for I want to emphasise the way in which the pace and tone of the writing has slowed for the last moments of Richard Beattie-Seaman's life. It's a relatively crude but effective ploy. The repetition of words and sounds – 'pain', 'rain', 'dying', 'cool' – and the insistence of the

' . . ing' ending of words, also contribute to the sombre winding down of the poem.

2   *Speak the poem to myself.*

I had been sounding out this poem during its composition, but it was only after a first public reading of the piece that I realised how difficult it was to perform the poem at the right pace and with the correct emphasis. In fact, after including it in the first of a series of readings in America that year, I felt that I was not doing the poem justice and therefore withdrew it from the programme for the rest of that week. On my return I learned of the poem's success in the competition and was faced with the prospect of having to be interviewed about the poem and then reading it on a Radio Three broadcast. I found that I could best cope with the demands of the poem by rediscovering the feelings of empathy for Richard Beattie-Seaman and the deep irony I felt for his predicament. In a sense one had to become Seaman, rather, I suppose, as an actor might. Though, lacking any experience or skill in that direction, no doubt I fell short of that aim.

It is, nevertheless, always an interesting and constructive exercise to place oneself in the position of a character in any literary text. We do this, I think, when we enjoy many novels and films. As a reader, I also find it useful, when faced by a difficult poem, to imagine that I had to direct a film of the scene contained in the poem. If I can visualise actions in specific space and hear speech along with an impression of the facial and physical gestures of the speaker, then I find that I can understand many poems more readily. I feel that our schools and colleges attach too little importance to that business of lifting the poem off the page. Why should poems be any less dramatic or watchable than plays?

The Death of Richard Beattie-Seaman in the Belgian Grand Prix, 1939 was still causing me concern as I practised my reading on the train up to London. No doubt it was causing some concern also to my fellow-passengers! Principally, I was coping with the bulk of the poem, but unsure about the ending. Was it to be a Big Ending, full of significance? I read it that way in the studio rehearsal – quietly progressing through the first three lines of the last section, and then pronouncing with as much significance as I could the last line. BBC producer Fraser Steel heard and pointed out immediately the folly of this. He argued that if the words work, if the poem as a whole has worked, then the last line will insist its point without any theatrical effects. I should, he suggested, deliver 'engines roaring' with more volume, and then come down to a normal level for 'as at the start of a great race', allowing the ambiguity of those words to sink it under their own weight.

Frankly, it was only after having absorbed that point that I realised how insecure I had been about the poem. My worries concerning the prosaic delivery of information at certain points, and of the possible confusion listeners and readers might experience as the poem shifts in time, were, in a sense, redeemed if the ending were delivered with confidence. The time switches and the variation in the mood as Seaman's experiences change could be delivered positively if I could only trust to the score of the piece, the stage directions indicated by the structure of the poem. Therein lies also the answer to the question –

3   *What patterns can I see in the poem?*

As I argued in response to Adrienne Rich's *Translations* in Chapter 1, the overriding principle of organisation in the poem is that narrative impulse to push down the page to some conclusion or resolution of the elements of the story. However, there was, as I have indicated, a considerable awareness in the composition of the poem that I needed to employ the poet's 'tricks of the trade', the devices of alliteration, rhyme, para-rhyme and variation of pace, those means of foregrounding the language of the text at the same time that I was unfolding the narrative. Where rhymes offered themselves, then I worked to incorporate them; where a line flowed and suggested alliteration, then I chose to alliterate. Key words are repeated, as we have seen. There is parallelism too. But perhaps the most obvious poetic dimension in this text is the imagery, the figures of speech. And a consideration of that imagery leads inevitably to our fourth point.

4   *Discuss any ambiguities or paradoxes in the poem.*

The central ambiguity is that which drew me first to the story of Richard Beattie-Seaman, and then to commit myself to a poem. I felt sure that there was more than one possible meaning embodied in the story. Just as the huge efforts which Nazi Germany and other countries committed to motor racing and the Schneider Trophy air races of the period were not entirely motivated by a sporting interest and a deep-rooted sense of competitive fair play, so I felt that Seaman's death was not simply the loss of an English ex-public schoolboy who had paid the price for his playboy indulgence in fast cars. I could not forget that back in Britain at that time there was mass unemployment and that working-class children in many areas of the country were malnourished, badly housed, some of them suffering the diseases of poverty such as rickets. And yet at the end of that decade of the 1930s, a few months after the Belgian Grand Prix in which Seaman died, men such as he, with the privilege of a flying licence, were to form the core of Churchill's 'Few', the saviours of Western civilisation, no less.

Richard Beattie-Seaman was himself aware of the strangeness of his position as the true nature of the Third Reich revealed itself. He contacted the Foreign Office in London for advice after the German Grand Prix win: should he remain on the Continent driving for Mercedes? The reply was that he was serving his country well by his success on the racing circuit and should continue to race, at least for the time being.

That sense of irony is worked for in my re-creation of his famous victory. His great win, in front of an enormous crowd, the culmination of that feeling of supreme confidence and well-being as he flew over the scene, all that is undercut by the fluttering swastikas, the constant, overseeing presence of Korpsfuhrer Hehnlein, the obligatory 'Hitlergruss' on the victory rostrum. There was the newspaper headline 'An Englishman the toast of Germany!' and the formal, smiling reception of Adolf Hitler at the Mercedes works.

Given a situation as complex, and an historical moment so crucial as this, the mining and refining of images was not difficult. Simply retelling events with some attention to detail would, I felt, have surely engaged the attention of readers. As I began to retrieve freely, imaginatively the experiences of Richard Beattie-Seaman, I found that the layers of paradox, of a cruel irony, were clearly revealed.

First, there is the paradox of a racing driver immobilised

and dying in a machine built for speed and sporting entertainment. Then there is the weather; Richard Beattie-Seaman
burns to death because there is too much water that day. The
track gleams attractively, but has the effect of a cutting blade.
The flames 'flowering' from the engine in front of him have a
strange beauty. His memory of Rugby and the ordered world
of morning services in a private chapel, the close warmth of
sunshine through the windows, both reassuring and stifling, was,
presumably, the sort of existence which he was escaping by his
choice of such a dangerous sport. They return to release him from
present torment. The wreath of victory placed around his neck at
Nurburgring is a portent of the funeral wreath won in Belgium.
The Hitlergruss becomes the waves of excitement and then panic
as he crashes the following year. The quiet, edged with distant
roarings, is both his escape and his fate at the poem's close. He
has crashed at *La Source*, where water springs from the ground,
the source of life itself. Earth, air, fire and water conspire at his
death.

It may seem that such an exercise as that is somewhat stilted
when performed by the poet himself. Does that really represent
a summary of my responses to the poem?

Or is it unlikely that poets would be able to detach themselves
from a piece objectively, so as to be able to construct a convincing
critical view?

I think that I can view this particular poem with a sufficient
degree of detachment and objectivity, because it is a researched,
'worked for' piece. Whilst feeling an affinity for Richard Seaman,
I am just as concerned to explore and re-create some of the history
of that period. I want to suggest the uneasy atmosphere, the slid-
ing away of innocence in the face of the portents of impending
destruction which the 1930s laid down. I am sympathetic towards
Seaman, an individual trapped at the most tragic point of human
affairs in this century. And yet I can see that, in another sense,
he is a character acting out a part in events as distant as an old
newsreel.

I have written poems which dealt with personal loss, the death
of parents, of friends, pain and emotional stress closer to home.
In a sense it was to counterbalance several years of writing such
confessional poetry as it may be termed, that I decided in the
early 1980s positively to explore historical material, particularly
stories and characters from the two world wars. I have always

believed that poetry should be able to deal with the full range of human emotions, and dramatic possibilities; that poetry should not be confined to the short lyric. Surely after a while it becomes a strain, and possibly embarrassing, to be playing the role of the sensitive being at the centre of a confused universe?

But, you might argue, haven't you simply grafted that role on to an historical character? Haven't you elaborated on a set of facts and loaded your Beattie-Seaman with a seriousness and representational weight which he may not have had?

Well, I am relying on the tension between historically determinable fact and imaginative involvement to carry the work off successfully. The documentary nature of the title and the, I trust, convincing degree of detail concerning the race and of the sport in general work to legitimise the feelings and emotions which I invest in the character of Richard Beattie-Seaman himself. I am relying, too, on the tension between that individual character and the wider political context of the late 1930s, so that the whole will weave an engaging and convincing story in poetry form.

I am considerably more confident in my public reading of this poem now. For a year or so after the National Poetry Competition I felt I had to include it in all my readings. (It was, often, the reason for the invitation to read at festivals and other literary events.) I must confess to feeling more enthusiastic when reading some other poems from that period of my writing: there's 'From the City that Shone' about two young soldiers enjoying a brief, peaceful interlude in Flanders in the Great War and a poem called 'Soup', suggested by a story in one of Elie Wiesel's remembrances of Auschwitz. The poem on which I am currently working is 'Friedhof'. It was begun following a recent visit to Belgium, and, particularly, to Ypres – the town the British Tommies called 'Wipers' in Flanders; so you can see that poets may pursue their subjects or themes over a number of poems and years just as a novelist will explore a character or society through a long novel or sequence of novels.

I would also like to point out that it is not always fair or constructive to characterise a poet in terms of a single poetic strategy or to generalise about themes. Such themes are as often determined by critics, for they have a habit of tidying up the cluttered and eclectic lives and work of writers and artists. In my own defence, too, I would also wish to record that over the previous year I have completed poems on the following subjects:

the death of my 93-year-old Uncle Charlie; memories of working in a bread factory when I was a student; Auguste Rodin the sculptor; a strange conversation overheard in a hotel in west Wales; the ostracisation of a gay man in a train; going to a rugby match with my son. If there are critics interested, then I challenge them to draw straightforward conclusions from that selection!

Remember, whenever you study a poet, you are always working from someone else's selection of the work. It is always interesting to take the time and trouble to find out which poems the editor (even if it be the poet himself) had left out. What you make of *The Death of Richard Beattie-Seaman in the Belgian Grand Prix, 1939* is, of course, for you, the reader, to judge for yourself. The poet in me, however, should now withdraw to a safe distance, while the critic moves on to the next chapter and the next decades: the 1940s and 1950s.

3

The 1940s and 1950s

THE political and military pressures woven around the world of motor racing in which Richard Beattie-Seaman died finally conspired to bring war to Europe a few months after his death. The Second World War changed everyone's life and dominated the writing of the 1940s. I want to look at some poems from the direct experience of war, as well as poetry which reflected the experience of the home front. In particular I want to look at the following poems, using the same steps as previously:

All Day it has Rained, by Alun Lewis
Vergissmeinnicht, by Keith Douglas
A refusal to mourn the death, by fire, of a child in London, by
   Dylan Thomas
A Peasant, by R. S. Thomas.

The first poem, by Alun Lewis, deals with the experience of war as a rather distant, threatening thing. He is bored at his training camp and longs for action, no matter how acute the danger may be. By contrast, Keith Douglas writes out of his active service in the desert war against Rommel; he reacts to the probable fate of all soldiers, whatever uniform they wear. Both of these men find, like the soldier poets of the First World War, that the experiences of war galvanise them into a new-found creative strength. In fact, it is likely that their reading of poems from that previous war, as well as those produced by the poets of the Thirties who passionately espoused the cause of the Left in Spain, also informed their work. Lewis and Douglas were acutely aware of their role as soldier poets, but were conscious, too, of the precedents of quality which had been set by earlier poets, from Owen and Sassoon to Auden and Spender. Dylan Thomas, a civilian through the war, and already a poet with a considerable reputation, composes an

elegy for a victim of the Blitz. R. S. Thomas, a vicar in rural
Wales, writes in response to the harsh life of his parishoners
isolated, it seems, from change, progress and world events.

I

ALL DAY IT HAS RAINED
by Alun Lewis

All day it has rained, and we on the edge of the moors
Have sprawled in our bell-tents, moody and dull
    as boors,
Groundsheets and blankets spread on the muddy
    ground,
And from the first grey wakening we have found
No refuge from the skirmishing fine rain   5
And the wind that made the canvas heave and flap
And the taut wet guy-ropes ravel out and snap.
All day the rain has glided, wave and mist and
    dream,
Drenching the gorse and heather, a gossamer stream
Too light to stir the acorns that suddenly   10
Snatched from their cups by the wild south-westerly
Pattered against the tent and our upturned dreaming
    faces.
And we stretched out, unbuttoned our braces,
Smoking a Woodbine, darning dirty socks,
Reading the Sunday papers – I saw a fox   15
And mentioned it in the note I scribbled home;-
And we talked of girls, and dropping bombs on
    Rome,
And thought of the quiet dead and loud celebrities
Exhorting us to slaughter, and the herded refugees;
– Yet thought softly, morosely of them, and as
    indifferently   20
As of ourselves or those whom we
For years have loved, and will again
Tomorrow maybe love; but now it is the rain
Possesses us entirely, the twilight and the rain.

And I can remember nothing dearer or more to my
    heart   25
Than the children I watched in the woods on Saturday
Shaking down burning chestnuts for the schoolyard's
    merry play,
Or the shaggy patient dog who followed me
By Sheet and Steep and up the wooded scree
To the Shoulder o' Mutton where Edward Thomas
    brooded long   30
On death and beauty – till a bullet stopped his song.

1   *What sort of writing is shaped in front of me?*

This is a poem in two sections: the first comprises 24 lines and
the second 7 lines. Noting that sort of structure, I feel that it is
reasonable to presume that the experiences presented in the first
section will in some way be extended significantly, or summarised,
or contrasted, or even contradicted by the second section.

2   *Speak the poem to myself.*

My initial impressions are that the poem is a pleasure to read:
there are no difficulties with obscure diction, no tongue-twisting
configurations. There is, however, some work to be done to pace
oneself through the poem. That first section is a longish piece of
writing and the lines are uniformly long; longer than any of the
lines which we have encountered so far in any of the poems in
this book, with the exception of the Shakespeare sonnet. Again,
there are only four sentences in the whole poem – three in the
first section, while the second section forms a single sentence.
Relatively few of the lines are end-stopped by punctuation; many
more are run-on lines. Having said that, there is no sense of the
poem making unnecessary or unreasonable demands upon the
reader. Each line, each sentence is firmly punctuated. In fact,
many of the lines have a sense of being balanced, of being in two
parts. This pause or break in the flow of a sentence which affects
meaning and emphasis is called a *caesura*, and may be signalled by
punctuation or a conjunction or simply by the reader's response to
the sense of the line. So, for example, the first line of this poem has

a pivotal point indicated by the comma before 'and'; the second also by a comma; the third by the sense of 'Groundsheets and blankets/ spread on the muddy ground'.

3   *What patterns can I see in the poem?*

Obviously, this poem has no verses; its two sections at a first reading resemble two paragraphs of prose fiction. The first steadily builds up a list of impressions, some of them in particular detail, while the second seems to instance a memory which the poet wants the reader to associate with what has gone on previously. I want, at first, to stress the detailed impressionism of the poem, rather than the narrative impulse. It is the particularity of experience which I find most striking at this stage of my reading, though I have a sense, as yet unresolved, that the poem does have a narrative and thematic destination. The extent and intensity of these impressions is skilfully organised by the poet. Alun Lewis uses rhyme in a very clever way to guide and control his reader's response to the poem. I shall now look at rhymes in more detail.

At first sight (and sound) the poem seems to be composed of rhyming couplets. The rhymes are strong, masculine rhymes. That is to say, Lewis chooses words which form full rhymes with just the single, final syllables rhyming; for example, moors/boors, home/Rome, again/rain. 'Rain – that's the key word of the poem, obviously. But, perhaps less obviously, the first 'rain' in line 5 is separated from its rhyme by sixteen lines and eight pairs of other rhymes. As if to emphasise that gap, the matching rhyme of 'again' is followed by the repetition of 'rain' in the closing couplet of the first section. It is noticeable too that the first line of the second section chooses not to match 'heart' with a rhyme, though English offers a host of possibilities. The irregularity of these aberrations must serve a deliberate purpose, for Lewis has exhibited his skill and dexterity in employing rhyme through the body of the poem. It would be facile to suggest that his imagination and control must have left him at these two odd moments in the poem. Surely these points serve to indicate that Alun Lewis wants to vary the predictability of the rhyming couplet. By 'spoiling' the pattern, both visual and aural, he is disturbing the surface of the poem, not allowing the words and their images, or, for that matter, the reader to settle. The poem, after all, is about boredom, the predictability of a regimented training camp and the echoing predictability of the constant rain. And yet, that predictability is the calm before the storm. It represents an eerie, perhaps sham, normality preceding the turmoil of war. The rhyming scheme and the exceptions to its regularity are, then, both deliberate and effective. Such a strategy should alert us to expect several layers and forms of ambiguity in this poem.

The other strong sense of patterning in the poem is created by Lewis's poetic rhythm. We have noted that these lines are as long, and sometimes longer, than Shakespeare's in 'Shall I compare thee to a Summer's day?'. However, Lewis does not employ the regularity of the iambic pentameter. In order to describe his use of rhythmic patterns we will need to talk about the stress given to certain words, together with the use of pauses, *caesura*, and the pace at which the narrative flows. As I have already noted, many of these lines work to set up a balance of information and imagery. This is quite clearly the case in the first four lines which I read with a pivotal pause at, respectively, 'rained,' and 'bell-tents,' and 'blankets' and 'wakening'. Then, at line 5 I feel myself being accelerated through to the 'fine rain', and then, after a slight line-end pause, accelerated through the last two lines of the first sentence. The effect of the rhythm and pacing of these opening lines is to accentuate the mood which the poet wishes to create. The boredom and immobility of the situation combine with the relentless attack of the elements. Of course, other factors contribute to the effect. The long vowel-sounds of 'moors', 'sprawled', 'moody', 'boors' and 'muddy' succeed in dragging down the pace and the mood. Notice, though, how the short monosyllables of lines 6 and 7 quicken with the effect of the wind. At line 8 the repetition of 'All day' sets up another sequence of slow movements becoming, after the pause in line 9, a quicker, windier experience.

Those effects take place within or against a basic rhythmic pattern which I perceive as a six-stress line. This works with three stressed words or syllables either side of the pause. So, the first three lines of the poem may be illustrated in the following way:

All day it has **rained**, / and **we** on the **edge** of the **moors**
Have **sprawled** in our **bell-tents**, / **moody** and **dull**
        as **boors**,
Groundsheets and **blankets** / **spread** on the **muddy ground**

Of course, this pattern of stresses becomes varied as the poet shifts his attention and mood; there are a number of lines with five stresses, and some with just four, particularly as the first section ends and the poet comes to an albeit brief realisation of the place of love within the war in which he finds himself. In any analysis of a poem we must be prepared to comment on the rhythm where we perceive parallels and patterns. We may not have time exhaustively to outline the stresses of each line, but it is likely that where there is a measured feeling to the poetry we will hear that effect in our reading of the poem. Further, we will realise that the rhythm of the poem will be a strong factor in the execution of the poet's purpose.

4 *Discuss any ambiguities or paradoxes in the poem.*

The central paradox in this poem is the fact that a civilian conscripted into a wartime army should find himself so bored, and consider himself so peripheral to the momentous events of the time. This routine boredom and the predictability of the petty demands that the camp makes are underlined by the very full rhymes of the couplets. However, as we have noted, the occasional interruption of that rhyming pattern serves to remind the reader that this scene represents a false security. The rain is 'skirmishing' rather than refreshing; it rides on a wind that pulls at their shelter, threatens to snap the ropes which secure. Drifting into dreams, Lewis and his fellow soldiers are hit by acorns, the seeds of a promise they will probably never realise in their lives. For the present their lives are certainly banal – 'unbuttoned our braces, / Smoking a Woodbine, darning dirty socks, / Reading the Sunday papers – ' though the sighting of a fox (note that near-comic rhyming with 'dirty socks') is remarkable, a reminder of the countryside and worth a mention in the 'scribbled' note home. The underlying ambiguity, an ambiguity which is sustained right up to line 17, is that one is not absolutely positive that the narrator is in the army. Until we reach that line which ironically rhymes 'home' with 'Rome' we might well be assuming that the camp was a work or scout camp. That ambiguity is resolved by the eight lines at the end of the first section, though the resolution carries a great weight of irony: in the pairing of rhymes such as 'celebrities' and 'refugees'; in the critical balancing of lines such as 'And we talked of girls, and dropping bombs on Rome,'; in the assonance which ties 'Exhorting' to 'slaughter'; in the extension of that slaughter to the 'herded' refugees.

At the close of that first section perhaps the strongest challenge to the reader is that of the poet's self-deprecating criticism. We have been drawn into a relationship with the poet and feel a sympathy for these conscripts and the predicament in which they find themselves. Yet we are confronted by the apparently careless and cruel talk of the men, and then by the numbness of their emotions. Our feelings may well be ambiguous after a first reading; the extent to which we may feel prepared to empathise with the poet and his companions may well be limited. However, a reading which emphasised the shallow bravado of line 17 and which then stressed the irony of lines 18 and 19 would prepare the way for the underlying tone of sorrow occasioned by the 'morose' thoughts of the fate of the innocent victims in war and the poet's realisation that one needs to suspend one's empathy and love during active service. Love has been possible in the past, it may be again possible after the war, but for the present it is effectively washed away by the rain.

The second section is no less challenging or perplexing. At first it may seem as if the present tense of the poem has been changed or compromised by the opening line:

And I can remember nothing dearer or more to my heart

The first section has been presented in the perfect tense. That recall of events as a present experience is fairly commonly used by poets for it creates an immediacy that grips the reader. In fact, the second section is continuing that tense, for line 26 locates the memory in the recent past, the preceding day, Saturday. However, the warmth and emotional charge which he derives from, successively, schoolchildren knocking down conkers and 'the shaggy patient dog' seems, at first, strange and unjustified following on from his suspension of powerful feelings under the insistent rain. This ambiguity may be resolved though if one accepts the poet's mood. In the face of imminent oblivion the fact of his love for those closest to him is too much to bear. Rather, he fixes his emotions on two apparently casual encounters. Each of these is worth pausing over. First, the children's game must evoke memories of his own autumns of innocence. In fact, one could argue that his judgement in choosing the rather laboured '*merry* play' has been swayed by the very force of that recollection. Second, the dog offers an uncomplicated, unthinking obedience, close to, or easily taken for a sort of love. The dog follows Lewis as he climbs the colourfully-named Shoulder o' Mutton, making what is almost a pilgrimage to that spot where an 'Edward Thomas brooded long / On death and beauty'. Whoever this Edward Thomas might be, he is clearly admired by Lewis and has obviously met a violent and premature death himself.

Edward Thomas might well have been personally known to the poet. He may have been murdered. Neither of those suppositions is unjustifiable or absurd. However, we must ask ourselves whether a poet who has been at such pains to create a detailed set of impressions in the body of the poem would end by going off at a tangent and confusing us by an obscure reference. Is the poem to be no more than a shaggy patient dog story? It is unlikely. Alun Lewis clearly expects many of his readers to recognise the name Edward Thomas. Now, if you do not recognise Edward Thomas as the poet killed, like so many other men, in the 1914-18 war; if you do not know that Thomas yearned to be a true Welshman, compulsively travelling in and writing about Wales, then are you going to be disastrously, and unfairly penalised in your written response to this poem? Of course not. If you did know those facts, then, naturally, you will be able to impress an examiner. But if you are faced by a name you don't recognise, then try to make a sensible guess from the poem's content. Logically, a reader should be able to reason that, as this poem is about war and the probability of death in war, then the reference at the critical point of the poem's conclusion to 'Edward Thomas' must be contributing to that theme. Thomas must have died in battle. That battle would probably have been fought in either the Spanish Civil War (1936-39) or in the First World War. And, just as probably, Alun Lewis, himself morosely brooding in the rain, is prefiguring his own death; another poet in another war whose 'song' is stopped.

5   *Summarise my responses to the poem.*

This is a wartime poem (written, in fact, in 1941) in which Alun Lewis succeeds in creating a very special feeling of sadness and protest. He protests at the political events which have tumbled the world into war; the conflicts of ideas and the breakdown of normal human values which have resulted in 'slaughter, and the herded refugees'. At the same time it is the sadness of the immediate situation in which Lewis and his fellow soldiers have been placed which is most vividly evoked in the poem. The whole poem builds on a series of ambiguities and paradoxes, small ironies such as 'acorns that suddenly . . . / Pattered against the tent and our upturned dreaming faces' which clearly portend larger issues and suffering. The significance of small happenings is magnified, thrown into relief by the wider context of the war which these men are soon to join. And yet the poet, throughout the long first section, holds back from the full emotional charge of his feelings. It is as if the rain is constantly diluting the power to engage with and fully care about those larger issues.

In the second section Lewis seems to be detaching himself from the immediacy of those issues with his tangential references to the schoolchildren and the dog. However, the final couplet pins those images down and locates in them what T. S. Eliot called an 'objective correlative' for the powerful emotions within the poet. That is, Alun Lewis fixes his sorrow and anger on two images of human value – the innocence of childhood and the affectionate dog which follows him to 'the Shoulder o' Mutton', a place which Lewis associates with one of his poet-heroes, Edward Thomas, a man who was also overtaken by fateful events larger than his own life.

All Day it has Rained is a challenging, but rewarding poem. It has strong lyric and narrative qualities, mixing the banal with the intensely felt moment – those complex experiences which are peculiar to war. Alun Lewis succeeds in conveying the ordinary feelings of a soldier at a rest or training camp, but he achieves that in a uniquely poetic way. His skilful use of the rhyme scheme, the run-on line, the balancing of individual lines and the rhythmic variations in his writing all contribute to a memorable poem, the climax to which is surprisingly abrupt and profoundly moving.

II

VERGISSMEINNICHT
by Keith Douglas

Three weeks gone and the combatants gone,
returning over the nightmare ground
we found the place again, and found
the soldier sprawling in the sun.

The frowning barrel of his gun
overshadowing. As we came on
that day, he hit my tank with one
like the entry of a demon.

Look. Here in the gunpit spoil
the dishonoured picture of his girl
who has put: *Steffi. Vergissmeinnicht*
in a copybook gothic script.

We see him almost with content,
abased, and seeming to have paid
and mocked at by his own equipment
that's hard and good when he's decayed.

But she would weep to see today
how on his skin the swart flies move;
the dust upon the paper eye
and the burst stomach like a cave.

For here the lover and killer are mingled
who had one body and one heart.
And death who had the soldier singled
has done the lover mortal hurt.

(*Vergissmeinnicht* is the German for 'forget-me-not'.)

1   *What sort of writing is shaped in front of me?*

This is a poem of 24 lines, formed of 6 quatrains. For the most
part these quatrains follow the rules of conventional punctuation and grammar. However, there are no capital letters at the

beginning of lines. Two foreign words (I am told they are German) are included, and these are italicised. I do not recognise this poem as any traditional form, but the fact that it progresses in such an ordered manner will, no doubt, be an important factor in both my reading and my analysis of the text.

2 *Speak the poem to myself.*

I find this poem quite straightforward to read. The shorter lines seem less demanding than, say, some of those in the Alun Lewis poem. Each verse is comprised of one or two sentences and none runs on into the following verse. This means that one may read the poem in an accommodating, measured way. Having said that, there are instances where the line-ending is a firm indication of punctuation though none is given. The fourteenth line is an obvious example of that effect. I found myself pausing for slightly longer after that line than the remaining three in that verse. On the other hand, lines such as lines 3 and 6 and 15 demand to run on into the following line in order to exemplify meaning and vary the pace of the poem.

I am aware that a poem of six quatrains rhyming, say, *abab*, *cdcd*, and so on, would set up a pattern ideal for a longer narrative, or for humour, or satire; but this regular rhyme scheme would be too reassuringly obvious for the subject matter of 'Vergissmeinnicht'. The way in which Keith Douglas had varied the order of his rhymes feels and sounds interesting and is, I think, appropriate to the disturbing nature of his poem. The fact that the rhythm and the degree of rhyming are also varied is striking and will surely reward further thought when I pose my next question.

3 *What patterns can I see in the poem?*

I have noted the obvious typographical uniformity of this poem, but have already suggested that there are various ways in which Douglas is refusing to regulate his poem in an absolute way. He will not allow the eye or the ear of the reader to settle into an expectation of rhyme or a regularity of rhythm. His line-ending rhymes are various and, at times, ambiguous:

abba
aca(?)c or caac(?) or acca(?)
ddee(?)
fgfg
hih(?)i(?)
jkjk(?)

There is a sense in which the middle verses settle into a more predictable pattern, but that possibility is firmly denied by the poet's use of half-rhymes such as 'move' / 'cave' and 'heart' / 'hurt'. These pairings are very reminiscent of the para-rhymes which the First World War poet Wilfred Owen used so originally and brilliantly in his poem 'Strange Meeting'. There is also the further complication of *internal rhyme* that is the rhyming of a line-ending word with another in the middle of a line. For example, 'ground' in line 2 rhymes with 'found' in line 3 *before* it is matched by another 'found' at the end of that line. Again, 'Look' at the beginning of line 9 rhymes with 'copybook' in the middle of the last line of the third verse. All these variations on the standard use of rhyme contribute to the constant unease which the poet wants to maintain within the organising framework of his poem.

I can perceive no regularity of rhythm in this poem. The lines vary in their stressed words and syllables, but generally stress three or four words. There are parallel stress patterns though, in some of the pairings of rhymed lines. For example:

who had one body and one heart

and

has done the lover mortal hurt,

Keith Douglas is running his line over the tracks of a metrical four-beat iambic base. Again, the point to be made is that this poem never allows such a patterning to establish itself. The poem is addressing the ways in which the horror of war perverts natural human experiences and priorities; the theme is underpinned by the refusal to accept those devices of poetic order which both the poet and his reader know are possible.

4   *Discuss any ambiguities or paradoxes in the poem.*

Of course, the title is probably ambiguous for most English readers. We will recognise it as a German word, simply from the sound, particularly that characteristic *icht* ending. But why would Keith Douglas use such a word and risk confusing his readers? There must be a very compelling reason. If we can come to an explanation of that title, then surely we will be well on our way to locating the central purpose of the poem. In any anthology or examination paper in which we might encounter the poem, of course, the translation would be provided. That taken, we can begin to sound the word alongside the English 'forget-me-not'. Try doing that for yourself. There is a four-syllable rhythm common to both words which is obvious to the ear:

for*get*-*me*-not
Ver*giss* *mein* nicht

Keith Douglas is surely making the point that with the common, shared rhythm also go common, shared sentiments. Whatever the uniform worn the man beneath is a man with feelings and a need for love. We may not, after all, be necessarily divided by language, for if we really listen we will surely find that we share the same concerns, that we have the same things to say. The grim irony in this poem is that it is only by confronting the corpse of an 'enemy' soldier lying in the sand that Douglas is able to remind himself of that important fact and thus reinforce his belief in a common humanity.

There is a shocking pathos in the discovery of the photograph inscribed by Steffi, for, at once, Douglas is stressing the humanity of the dead German soldier and accusing him of dishonouring his love by his involvement in the war. This accusation overturns the conventional moral stance of the state which compels one to fight as the highest expression of one's love for country and kin. The ambiguity lies in the nature of 'dishonoured', for it could be taken that the British army has dishonoured this instance of love by killing the German gunner, but that, I think, would be to narrow the import of Keith Douglas's message.

I encounter some difficulty in reading the second verse. The first sentence of that second verse is, grammatically speaking, not a sentence. I have to work to visualise the scene as discovered by Keith Douglas. I see the sprawling soldier sheltered from the sun by the shadow of the gun. But it is a 'frowning' gun, an instrument of war which, rather than protecting him, has, ironically, brought about his death. It has blocked out the sun. I suppose that the 'one' of the third line is a shell. But, clearly, Douglas's tank was not severely damaged because the implication is that he was able to retaliate and silence both the gunner and his anti-tank gun. It is also possible to read into that sentence the change wrought upon Douglas himself by the direct hit on his tank. It is as if from that moment a demon enters him and he fights back to kill.

There are several words which occasion comment. In the first verse 'sprawling' is, momentarily, ambiguous. It is as if he is lazing in the sunshine, at leisure, out of the war, which, in the darkest sense, he is. 'Copybook gothic script' in the third verse might strike one at first as an odd detail. It is the laborious heavy style used in formal lettering and yet here it is the loving inscription from his lover on her photograph. I think we are meant to read into this the best-writing care which Steffi has put into the inscription. The Goths were one of the fiercest Germanic warrior tribes. It is ironical that this 'gothic' script should now serve as an inscription at the place of his death in a German army uniform.

5   *Summarise my responses to the poem.*

This is a poem from the experience of war which, like so many war poems, is really an anti-war poem. From the details of the sun and the flies I take this to be an incident in the desert war, and Douglas to be part of the British Eighth Army fighting Field Marshal Rommel for the control of North Africa. In the heat of battle, Keith Douglas has no option but to silence the anti-tank gun which has already come close to killing him. The action of the battle caries him on and it is only three weeks later that he is confronted with the reality of his retaliatory action. In that time the gunner's body has badly decomposed; his stomach has burst 'like a cave' and his skin is covered by blood-darkened, that is, by swarthy flies. His eyelids are paper-thin under the heat of the sun. In the process of decomposition the 'lover and killer are mingled'. The physical rooting of both aspects (and they are, surely, opposed aspects) of this man has meant that both are now lost in the broken body. In this 'nightmare' desert landscape he is mocked at by the metallic, relatively impervious weaponry and equipment; he dishonours the woman he loves by the squalor of his death. At once the climax of his sacrifice as a soldier, a killer, is negated by the pointless sacrifice of the lover who will no longer love or be the object of another's love.

By his control of the devices of rhyme and rhythm and the relentless pacing of his verse structure, by his personal response to the consequences of his action, Douglas has presented the reader with the horror of war and the immensity of an individual's moral responsibility in acts of warfare. His feeling of an unquestioning execution of a soldier's duties when he is, himself, under threat, is profoundly questioned and altered. He moves from a feeling of professional 'content' to a sobering statement of dignified regret in the last verse. His confrontation with the corpse that had been Steffi's lover is a horror which shakes Douglas. But he is left with the conviction that this cannot be the end for which mortal men were meant.

III

A REFUSAL TO MOURN THE DEATH, BY FIRE, OF A CHILD IN LONDON
by Dylan Thomas

Never until the mankind making
Bird beast and flower
Fathering and all humbling darkness
Tells with silence the last light breaking
And the still hour
Is come of the sea tumbling in harness

And I must enter again the round
Zion of the water bead
And the synagogue of the ear of corn
Shall I let pray the shadow of a sound
Or sow my salt seed
In the least valley of sackcloth to mourn

The majesty and burning of the child's death.
I shall not murder
The mankind of her going with a grave truth
Nor blaspheme down the stations of the breath
With any further
Elegy of innocence and youth.

Deep with the first dead lies London's daughter,
Robed in the long friends,
The grains beyond age, the dark veins of her mother,
Secret by the unmourning water
Of the riding Thames.
After the first death, there is no other.

1   *What sort of writing is shaped in front of me?*

This text is a poem of 24 lines, comprising 4 verses each of 6
lines. Each line begins conventionally with a capital letter and,
in addition to the regularity of the verse lengths, I can see that
the second and fifth line of each verse is shorter than the rest.
I have the immediate impression of a tightly structured poem
and expect to encounter the poet's thoughts and experiences in
a controlled and regulated way.

2   *Speak the poem to myself.*

Your first experience of reading this poem is likely to be,
like mine, a mixture of feelings – confusion, insecurity, intrigue,
amazement, may be just some of those initial responses. Even
after a second and third reading we may feel very uncertain
of the 'message' of this poem and the means by which Dylan
Thomas felt that he had to write it. The first point to stress is:
don't panic, remember to follow through the five steps which we
have seen work in setting up sensible and coherent responses to
other poems new to us.
    So, speaking the poem through to ourselves several times
because we don't feel that we have really engaged with the
text, is not an admission of some failure on the part of the
poet or ourselves. It is, instead, likely to be our first insight
into what the poem is setting out to do. Remember, we should
welcome some difficulties, some puzzlement when we encounter

a poem, or any work of art for the first time. That is the way art works, that is the way life works. Uncomplicated situations and messages or transparent situations and messages are the stuff of soap-operas and slogans.

The first reassuring aspect of this difficult poem is that it is written in grammatical sentences. There are four sentences, though as we saw in *Translations* and 'This is just to say' from Chapter 2, a sentence may cut across the division of a verse or section in a poem. That is the case in Dylan Thomas's poem and, because he chooses to run his first sentence across two verses to conclude with the first line of the third verse, he sets the reader a rather challenging task. There is, too, the consideration that he sets a series of quite testing images 'tumbling in harness' down the page in that first sentence. Again, the sentence has no commas by way of pause. We will, then, have to take the line-endings as strong indications of pause.

Now, when I speak the poem to myself again I can make a more confident progression through the first sentence and may begin to perceive the pace at which Thomas intends the reader to encounter this poem. From that basis I shall be much more aware and concerned about the sounds of these words. Dylan Thomas has written this poem with a richness of alliteration, assonance and rhyme the like of which we have not yet encounterd in this book. The length and sonority of the first sentence resounds with a biblical authority when you let the words perform themselves as the text indicates they should. There is also the *sense* of the opening words: 'Never until . . . ' – never until what? Discovering the subject and main verb of the sentence should hold the key to both its correct reading and the intention of the poem. The moment that we accept that the key to the sentence is in line 10 and 'Shall I let pray . . . ', then we begin to make sense of the syntax and may come closer to understanding the justification for such an apparently tortuous first half of the poem.

If Dylan Thomas has created a difficult poem, then it must be a very difficult subject that he wishes to address with that poem. The title proclaims his subject. What could be more agonising than the death of a child, a death by fire? And beyond that, what could be more unnatural, more indefensible than a refusal to mourn that death? Perhaps an examination of the structure of the poem may provide further illumination of some of these questions.

3   *What patterns can I see in the poem?*

I have already noted the verse lengths and the fact that the first sentence cuts across over half of the poem. The three remaining sentences are more readily contained by the verse structure, with the final line being the final sentence in complete contrast to the opening sentence. That move to conformity and clarity is surely crucial. The poem unravels a complex moral and emotional response which simply will not be contained by a conventional expression of grief. We can make that assumption with some confidence from a logical extension of the poem's structure.

Of course, our concentration on the sentence structure is emphasising the narrative and the development of the poet's argument. In a sense one has to shut out some of the layers of sound in order to perceive those aspects of the poem's structure. But it is the patterning of sound which is the overwhelming effect of the poem. Let us begin with the rhymes. These are full and strong, with Thomas employing both masculine and feminine rhymes: for example, 'round / sound' and 'making / breaking'. The rhyme scheme, in contrast to the syntax, begins quite predictably, but then becomes more slightly ambiguous in the second half of the poem.

> *abcabc*
> *defdef*
> *ghigh(?)i*
> *jkljk(?)l*

The complication of the consonant rhyme in the last verse increases the sense of uneasy connections between events, the feeling that there is, after all, a pattern to the tragic events themselves if we could but see it. The patterning is further enriched by internal rhyme – 'humbling / tumbling' and 'grains / veins', and the echoes of near-rhymes such as 'sea / valley' which, though separated by a verse, contribute to the obvious parallelism of their lines. It seems as if no opportunity to create alliterative effects and assonance has been missed. There could hardly be a clearer example than this poem of a writer whose aim is to foreground language, that is, to draw attention to language itself in equal part to the forward thrust of narrative or argument. The realisation that the language patternings of sound and rhythm are so central to Thomas's concerns must inform all our subsequent judgements of the poem. The rhythm varies through the poem, but I perceive the basic pattern to be a line of three strong stressed words established at the beginning of the poem, thus –

> **Never** until the **mankind making**
> **Bird beast** and **flower**
> **Fathering** and all **humbling darkness**

Now, three stressed lines or statements are the bread and butter rhetoric of both politicians and preachers. Try listening to a major statement or speech in a parliamentary broadcast and note the rhythm of that speech. Time and time again, you will be hearing words and phrases organised in triplets. It is not simply that every ambitious politician has studied the great, stirring wartime speeches of Winston Churchill, though it may strike you that the following serves as template for much that we have heard since: 'Never in the field of human conflict has **so much** been owed by **so many** to **so few**.' No, there is some special quality, some intrinsic force to the organisation of facts and arguments in sets of three. In this poem Thomas uses this fact to great effect and is quite prepared to further strengthen the pattern by adding alliteration, as in, 'Or **sow** my **salt seed**'. The overall effect of sounding out this poem is to enter and inhabit a veritable edifice of words and language which, like a cathedral, is solid in its construction and surprisingly varied in its contents.

4   *Discuss any ambiguities or paradoxes in the poem.*

We have already addressed the ambiguity of the poem's form. It is a tightly organised poem in rhyming verses which in its sentence structure cuts across that pattern to add a complexity of syntax and reasoning. The title gives a firm indication that this poem and its 'argument' will be ironically held by the poem and rhetorically presented to his reader. This will be an elegy which 'refuses to mourn'; it is an acceptance of the finality of death which, nevertheless, thunders its anger. It is a poem of sorrow, grief and stoicism. It blusters and blows the language which Thomas has culled from all the available sources of religion, society's way of organising personal joy and sadness, but deconstructs and remoulds that language and those images into an entirely original and uniquely personal response. It is a scream of anger and frustration that becomes a hard-won affirmation in its final line.

But before that final line we encounter rich layers of irony, a succession of striking metaphors. Take, for example, Thomas's use of the word 'mankind'. It is linked in the first line with 'making', as if the words are joined by a hyphen to emphasise the involvement, the blame carried by men in the fact of this death. What exactly has happened? Why is it important to know that this death has taken place in London? A death caused by man-made fire in London – doesn't that point to the probability that this is an incident from the Blitz? Those years in the Second World War when the Luftwaffe incessantly pounded the city as a means of softening up the British prior to Hitler's triumphant invasion? In fact, the great Churchill speech from which I quoted just now was the repudiation of that Nazi strategy. When 'mankind' is used again in line 15, 'The mankind of her going . . . ', it is in the more basic sense of our common mortality. Having said that, I think there is an ironic secondary meaning carried in both instances: I mean that in both warfare and in our natural mortality there is little kindness to be seen. In the first verse 'mankind making' prepares us for the following imagery of a life force bringing into being. 'Fathering', in fact, 'Bird beast and flower' as well as Mankind. There is, we must note, no direct reference to 'God' in the poem.

Thomas is proclaiming that until the last moment of existence – both *his* existence and Existence itself – he is determined not to mourn. Until he returns to 'the water bead' and 'the ear of corn' to the atom, the nothingness that precedes our individual existence, he will not publicly mourn. The 'Zion' (a name quite common in Welsh chapels) and the synagogue, with their ceremonies of grief, do not seem appropriate for the feelings he has. Public tears and sackcloth cannot approach 'The majesty and burning of the child's death'. What an ambiguous, almost shocking conjunction of feelings that line contains. I want to drop my voice at 'burning' to convey horror at the nature of her death. On the other hand, perhaps the word could be delivered equally effectively by an angry tone.

'Murder' in line 14 alliterates with 'majesty' and 'mankind', as well as 'mourn' from the previous verse, and this stress on that heavy, tight-lipped sound offers further evidence that anger is one of the principle emotions expressed in the middle of the poem. Anger would justify the heavy, punning irony of that 'grave truth', and prepares for the following line – 'Nor blaspheme down the stations of the breath' – one of the most striking images I have ever read. The transference of Christ's stations of the cross, the principle events of his tortured march to Golgotha and his crucifixion, to the notion that our breath, our life's journey, is but another progress to oblivion or salvation, that is a difficult but startling and highly original image.

Dylan Thomas refuses to mourn, refuses to write an elegy (traditionally, a poem in praise of a person at their death), so what is left to him? The last verse opens in as rich and sonorous a fashion as the poem's beginning. The three stressed 'd' sounds of 'Deep', 'dead' and 'daughter' sound out like the muffled tolling of a funeral bell. Her burial puts her to rest in the earth, 'The grains beyond age', succoured by the 'dark veins' of both her mother earth and her human mother's sorrow and pain. She is dispatched to a secret place, the grave's finality in stark contrast to the lively flowing waters 'Of the riding Thames'.

The final and perhaps most perplexing ambiguity in the poem is provided by its last line:

> After the first death, there is no other.

At first glance this line seems illogical. What could 'first' possibly have to do with 'death', for surely we all understand death to be the absolute finality. Thomas, we have seen, has constantly worked in the poem to deconstruct and re-form our understanding of language, the connotations of words. Thomas is not infrequently regarded as a 'difficult' poet. This, however, cannot be because he uses difficult, obscure words. His diction is far simpler, more elemental than many other poets. Take T. S. Eliot, for example, or Ezra Pound or our contemporary Geoffrey Hill, all of whom may make quite severe demands upon the reader and send us constantly back to the dictionary. No, the demands which Thomas makes upon his readers are of a different order. By transposing, switching words from their normal position in a sentence, by using them in a way which implies that they are a different part of speech, Dylan Thomas forces us to reconsider assumed meanings even of such a common word as death. In that last line he seems to be saying that, however tragic and unfair a blow may have been dealt by the child's violent death, each of us faces but one death. Death releases us as well as deprives us of life.

5   *Summarise my responses to the poem.*

This is a demanding poem which requires a considerable effort of reading and understanding on the part of the reader. However, it does address one of the most complex of life's challenges, the violent death of a child, one of the casual victims of modern war. Those very demands of syntax and imagery may, in fact, argue for the poem's unique ability to address such a subject. Faced by the enormity of such a loss, what might be achieved by a rational, logical response? Surely the rhetoric of Dylan Thomas's title and the astounding scope of his opening sentence provide the hard-won, appropriate response. The poem recognises the importance of our institutionalised responses to grief whilst holding to the belief that such public expressions are only ever the signals of a deeper sense of loss. It is a loss which is only partially assuaged by such actions. The ultimate significance of the child's death may be in the duality and ambiguity of the final, seemingly illogical and perhaps irrefutable statement. We have, finally, nothing to fear, for death is the natural end (and the only reward) for all our efforts. We return to our 'mother' but the 'unmourning water' flows by constantly, oblivious of our loss, or our words. At least, Dylan Thomas, seems to be saying, if we are to shout our anger and frustration and love into the wind, then let's make a memorable job of it.

IV

We have just looked at one of the remarkable poems produced by Dylan Thomas in the 1940s. He continued to write up to his premature death in 1953, though it must be said that he had begun many of his most memorable poems in the 1930s, when he was a very young man. The notebooks that survive from his nineteenth 'year to heaven' contain an astonishingly rich vein of originality that he was to mine for the rest of his life. Clearly it is unsatisfactory to summarise a writer's significance to a period of time, and certainly a relatively short period of time. I should therefore acknowledge that my division of this book into decades is an arbitrary one designed to enable readers to pace themselves through a number of the notable poems in the post-war period.

To conclude this chapter I want to look at a poem by R. S. Thomas which was written in the 1940s, but which reached a wide audience only in 1955 when a London publisher combined two earlier collections of Thomas's poems and produced *Song at the Year's Turning*.

Before I begin the critical analysis of Thomas's *A Peasant* it may be useful to offer a brief description of two developments in poetry in this period. In the 1950s a number of the poets writing in England became characterised as the 'Movement'; some others became known as the 'Group'. Put simply, the latter was a gathering under the direction of Philip Hobsbaum in Cambridge in 1952 of poets such as Alan Brownjohn, George MacBeth and Edward Lucie-Smith who felt that they could help each other's work. So useful did poets find the sessions of discussion and the 'workshop' of individual's poems in progress that these meetings continued in London into the 1960s. In 1963 Oxford University Press published *A Group Anthology* in which poems were collected, with Philip Hobsbaum adding a commentary on the practical workings of the 'Group'. On the other hand, the 'Movement' was the creation of several critics who perceived a common poetic strategy, common themes, a distinctive and reoccurring 'voice' in a significant number of poems published in the early years of the decade. It was an association of poets who shared a common style and attitude, rather than a physical means of collaboration. In fact, the 'Movement' was probably created by the *Spectator* magazine when in a leading article in 1954 it declared 'For better or worse, we are now in the presence of the only considerable movement in English poetry since the 'thirties . . . . It is bored by the despair of the 'forties, not much interested in suffering, and extremely impatient of poetic sensibility, especially poetic sensibility about *the writer and society* . . . The 'Movement', as well as being antiphoney, is anti-wet; sceptical, robust, ironic, prepared to be as comfortable as possible in a wicked, commercial, threatened world which doesn't look anyway as if it's going to be changed by a couple of handfuls of young English writers.'

Of course, poets want readers, they want to be taken notice of, and their publishers want their books to sell. The Movement poets sold (despite Charles Tomlinson's conviction that such poets exhibited a 'suburban mental ratio') and Philip Larkin, Donald Davie, D. J. Enwright and Elizabeth Jennings established reputations in the middle 1950s that have lasted to the present; while John Wain and Kingsley Amis have found equally lasting fame for their novels.

Literary fashions and debates were, in the 1950s, (not to say the 1980s) conducted in the quality national journals and newspapers; conducted, too, along an axis of power and taste that traditionally turned between Oxbridge and London even though more lasting and substantial writing was appearing to the north and west, and appearing, too, in Wales in the figure of R. S. Thomas to whom I now turn.

A PEASANT
by R. S. Thomas

Iago Prytherch his name, though, be it allowed,
Just an ordinary man of the bald Welsh hills,
Who pens a few sheep in a gap of cloud.
Docking mangels, chipping the green skin
From the yellow bones with a half-witted grin   5
Of satisfaction, or churning the crude earth
To a stiff sea of clods that glint in the wind –
So are his days spent, his spittled mirth
Rarer than the sun that cracks the cheeks
Of the gaunt sky perhaps once in a week.   10
And then at night see him fixed in his chair
Motionless, except when he leans to gob in the fire.
There is something frightening in the vacancy of
                                      his mind.
His clothes, sour with years of sweat
And animal contact, shock the refined,   15
But affected, sense with their stark naturalness.
Yet this is your prototype, who, season by season
Against the siege of rain and the wind's attrition,
Preserves his stock, an impregnable fortress
Not to be stormed even in death's confusion.   20
Remember him, then, for he, too, is a winner of wars,
Enduring like a tree under the curious stars.

1   *What sort of writing is shaped in front of me?*

This text is shaped as a poem of 22 lines. There are no divisions into verses or sections or paragraphs. Each line begins with a capital letter. There are no lines which stand out by their extreme length or shortness. I can immediately see some lines which rhyme, as the close conjunction of visually similar words imposes itself through the general impression of a block of writing, though I would be surprised to find an overall rhyme scheme in this poem.

2   *Speak the poem to myself.*

Well, that's a difficult opening line. 'Iago Prytherch' is quite a mouthful, sounds foreign and presents a challenge to the English speaker. I am helped, however, by the 'bald Welsh hills' of the next line, which locates the character and offers some assistance in my attempt to pronounce the man's name. It is not simply that name which creates a difficulty, however. The whole of the first line has a rather awkward feel. The syntax seems strained by the inversion of 'Iago Prytherch his name' followed by the oddness of ' . . . though, be it allowed'. Though I can see and hear the importance of the rhyme with 'cloud' in line 3. I am relieved that the sentence is a relatively short one. *A Peasant* is, at least, not making the same level of demands that we encountered in Dylan Thomas's *A Refusal to mourn*. Still, there is another demand made immediately, because the 'ordinary man' is described at work in a quite extraordinary way as he 'pens a few sheep', not in some stone or hedged enclosure, but in 'a gap of cloud'. The rhyme of lines 1 and 3 draws attention to the element of surprise, even shock, that the poet wishes to evoke from the reader. The second line is left hanging without a matching rhyme for 'hills', except that one can hear an imperfect internal rhyme with 'mangels' in line 4. Further on there are consonant links with 'grin', 'wind', and 'mind', but neither the ear nor the eye is allowed to settle into a security of expectation for too long in this poem, which mixes rhyming couplets with unrhymed lines and rhymes which are well distanced from their completing words. This unsettling effect should be considered with the fact that R. S. Thomas uses both alliteration, 'So are his days spent, his spittled mirth', and assonance, 'yellow bones', 'Enduring . . . curious', as a means of focusing our attention on the details and depth of his character as an object of our interest and concern.

That commitment to the text and our engaging with it by our rereading is the aim of every poet. Poetry, by its very nature, its foregrounding of language, is likely to demand more of us than many other forms of writing. That is what leads inexperienced readers to feel intimidated by the Poem. It is, though, also the reason why other people feel so enthusiastic about poetry. One should surely feel a quickening, an anticipation when language itself is worked into some fresh and intriguing form. In *A Peasant* R. S. Thomas describes a man who, frankly, is not exactly prepossessing. His physical appearance, his state of mind, his life-style (though that sounds too urban, bourgeois and anachronistic a term) as presented in the first sixteen lines of the poem are themselves strange, intimidating, even repulsive. It is only by stressing that 'Yet **this** is **your** prototype' that one can effectively prepare for the different sort of shock which awaits the reader in the poem's last six lines.

After the initial surprise of the opening line I would expect most readers to make a fairly confident reading of this poem. The long second sentence, from line 4 down to line 10 is broken and made manageable by the dash halfway through and the apparently unrhymed 'wind' which is completed only by the imperfect rhyme of 'mind' in the powerful image of line 13. As long as one realises the importance of 'So are his days spent . . . ' and 'Yet this is your prototype . . . ' to the pacing of the poem, *A Peasant* may be negotiated with a fair degree of ease, and, indeed, pleasure in the hard consonants of its verbs and adjectives such as 'Docking', 'clods', even 'gobs'.

3   *What patterns can I see in the poem?*

As I have noted, there is no overall rhyming scheme in the poem, but we can describe the pattern of its seven sentences:

> *aba*
> *ccdedff*
> *gg (?)*
> *h*
> *ih(?)j*

kkjk
ll(?)

so that it may be clearly seen that potential rhyme patterns are broken or imperfected, and that rhyming connections cross over sentences. There are two rhyming couplets, at lines 4 and 5 and 17 and 18, but these two serve only to emphasise the irregularity of the rest of the poem. It is the last six lines, when the poet is developing his argument and turning the reader around to a different set of considerations that the poem tightens its rhyming scheme – *kkjkll(?)* – so that the argument is effectively locked into the poem. We saw Shakespeare use the rhyming couplet to this effect in 'Shall I compare Thee to a Summer's day?' in Chapter 1. Here, R. S. Thomas is close to using only the second perfect masculine rhyme couplet of the poem as his conclusion. It is as if the effect he desires in *A Peasant* is that of the Petrarchan sonnet, except that it is a sixteen-line section of the poem which is countered and concluded by the final six lines.

That may be no more than conjecture, the critic grasping at straws and mud with which to wall in the poet's intentions. What I can feel certain of is that R. S. Thomas knows how a poem's structure works to shape and control both the poet's feelings and those to be evoked from the reader. He is evidently capable of rhyming whenever he wishes, full rhyme, consonant rhyme – 'chair / fire' – and internal rhyme. The fact that he chooses not to match all his line-endings is significant. It is significant, too, that he offers his reader vowel rhymes such as 'hills / skin / grin / wind' close to the assonance of 'chipping . . . -witted . . . stiff . . . glint . . . spittled', so that the early lines slip sharply into our awareness and penetrate our comfortable position as poetry readers. To further examine that feeling of unease which this poem creates, I need to go on to the next step of our analytical procedure.

4 *Discuss any ambiguities or paradoxes in the poem.*

The name 'Iago Prytherch', as we have noted, is the first ambiguity. The 'foreignness' of that name may have been resolved by the following line, but what is not resolved is the Shakespearean association of 'Iago'. Iago is the villain in Othello who tricks Othello and destroys his wife Desdemona because he feels he

has not been appreciated and promoted for his long service to
the state. He follows Othello ' . . . to serve my turn upon him',
proclaiming at the beginning of the play that

> We cannot all be masters, nor all masters
> Cannot be truly followed. You shall mark
> Many a duteous and knee-crooking knave
> That, doting on his own obsequious bondage,
> Wears out his time, much like his master's ass,
> For nought but provender; and when he's old, cashier'd.
>
> (I.i)

He ends that long speech by vowing to act the loyal friend, 'But
I will wear my heart upon my sleeve / For daws to pick at: I am
not what I am.'

Again, many readers might cry 'Unfair!' How is one to
pick up on every Shakespearean reference in a modern poet's
work? However, it may be argued that this is an instance where
such literary knowledge outside the poem might prove to be an
unwanted complication. The complexity of a character such as
Shakespeare's Iago seems quite unrelated to R. S. Thomas's hill
farmer. The latter is hardly involved in affairs of state, exhibits no
ambition, does not appear to be of consequence to any but himself
and the day-to-day running of his precarious sheep farm. Perhaps
that is precisely Thomas's purpose in naming him 'Iago', for there
is a great irony in burdening this seemingly insignificant man with
such connotations of intrigue, hatred and ambition. The first line
with its 'though, be it allowed' has the effect of undercutting the
seeming pretension of his parent's choice of names. Whatever
ambitions they may have held for Iago would appear to have
remained unrealised, despite their choice of a high-sounding
name culled from the family's *Complete Shakespeare* which was,
perhaps, together with the family bible, the only printed matter
on the farm. If one is unable to relate the farmer's name to the
Shakespearean character it is still quite obvious that the disparity
between that rather exotic name and the circumstances of the
farmer is significantly bound up with the poet's purpose.

But there is more to consider, for the third line seems to
shift the ground from under us once more. We may regard the
business of sheep farming in the Welsh hills to be a relatively
lowly occupation, but penning 'a few sheep in a gap of cloud'
is certainly a remarkable way of putting it. In the literal sense,

Iago has his head in the clouds. But it is his isolation rather than his vision which is being stressed, of course. He is trapped by the harshness of hill farming and the predictability of the cycle of work. He is one of the invisible workers and as the details of Iago Prytherch's working life are presented, we, too, are caught between the stultifying drabness of the menial tasks necessary to his survival and the peculiarity of the description. How much more effective and evocative a description of ploughing could one imagine than 'churning the crude earth / To a stiff sea of clods that glint in the wind?' It has the absolute conviction of closely-observed detail, yet avoids the sort of sentimental idealisation which some of the lesser Georgian poets exhibited in the years before the First World War.

If the description of Iago's working day is a contrast to the connotations of his name, then the piling on of negative, even repulsive detail has the effect of alienating the reader, leaving one unprepared for the final twist of the poem's conclusion. And that is precisely R. S. Thomas's purpose. The description of the farmer's work is consistently unpleasant. The mangels have 'green skin' and 'yellow bones' which Iago chips at like a dog at a corpse. His grin is 'half-witted', his mirth 'spittled' and rarer than sunshine which, in any case, 'cracks the cheeks / Of the gaunt sky'. Night brings an emptiness as he is 'fixed' in his chair, his mind vacant, his body smelling of 'sweat and animal contact', the inactivity broken by his move to 'gob in the fire'. The description has been unrelenting in its harshness, but while R. S. Thomas convinces us of the veracity of his observations, that comment on the state of Iago's mind must surely be questioned. When I took you through the drafts of my own poem in Chapter 2 I accepted that when I described Richard Beattie-Seaman's flight into Nurburgring and when I tried to explore the final moments of his consciousness trapped in that burning Mercedes racing car, that I had used (I hope not 'indulged in') imaginative, or 'poetic' licence. All writers do this. However, if we as readers feel that the character and sensations and sentiments occasioned by the writer seem to us to be unwarranted, unexplained, unjustified, then we must surely question the motives of that writer. Is R. S. Thomas not too harsh in his presentation of Iago Prytherch? Is not Iago a representative character, not merely an individual who embodies an aberration from the norm? Aren't we meant to take Iago as typical of a community's way of life? That being the case, where is the detail of a positive nature? We are not shown the market days, the cooperation between farmers in times of difficulty, at harvest-time, at lambing-time. Where is the social matrix of commerce, Church and entertainment which even the smaller towns of rural Britain offered, even in the immediate post-war years? If Iago Prytherch is an exception, an isolate who refuses or withdraws from social intercourse, then his strength as a representative figure is severely weakened.

A different emphasis may be made, however. A dissembling ambiguity and guile may not be the sole preserve of a Shakespearean villain. R. S. Thomas is surely working towards a reversal of our feelings in the final stage of the poem, and in order to make that reversal more dramatic he may be seen to draw his reader into sharing the extremes of repugnance which Iago's physical and mental states occasion in the poet. It is essential to this reading of the poem that we pay close attention to the particular and, I would argue, crucial ambiguity of lines 14, 15 and 16.

> His clothes, sour with years of sweat
> And animal contact, shock the refined,
> But affected, sense with their stark naturalness.

First, let us consider 'refined / But affected'. Surely Thomas is aiming this barb at those people who 'affect' refinement whilst retreating behind considerations of 'taste' and 'manners' in order not to have to confront the lot of the poor hill farmer. There is, though, another possible reading. He may be saying that his own feelings are ambiguous: on the one hand, he must admit his repugnance at the dereliction, the sweat, the stale animal smells, the dishevelled appearance of the farmer; on the other, Iago Prytherch is, nevertheless, a man in common with Thomas and with whomever else he may come into contact and Thomas may be admitting the fact that he is affected by this confrontation with his own basic humanity. Iago Prytherch, there before him within touching and smelling distance, imposes that realisation through the poet's veneer of civilised reserve. I think that the poem is strengthened by that ambiguity and profits from both those readings so that the 'Yet this is your prototype' of line 17 is addressed both to his audience and to the poet himself.

What we are encouraged, even forced, to acknowledge in the last six lines of the poem is that Iago Prytherch roots us to the reality of our past. All of us. 'Peasant' – the word is as much derogatory as descriptive for our society which has elevated itself beyond such a mode of livelihood. Peasants are rural dwellers who produce food for themselves, their families and little more than that. Such lives are a means of surviving, with little time or energy left for profiting from any surplus of produce. It might well be argued that the advance from such a self-sufficient base is the first step towards civilisation, with spare time and energy essential for the meditative and self-expressive activities of humans. Iago Prytherch, as R. S. Thomas portrays him, has no possibility for such advancement. Still, he is our 'prototype', our forerunner, our ancestor, though 'prototype' is a much more detached term than 'ancestor', and again rather disturbing in its cool distancing from the possibility of human empathy. It as if the poet is challenging us to involve our feelings with such a man. In fact, he immediately develops imagery which attributes the strength of buildings, castles, fortification to Iago. Like some fortified hill encampment he and his kind have withstood the assaults of the seasons' wind and rain. Not to be 'stormed' (there's such a telling ambiguity in that word) even by death. Now that is perplexing, for Iago has been presented to us as all too mortal a creature. I think that here lies the conclusive proof that R. S. Thomas has been developing the argument through the poem that Iago Prytherch *is* a representative, that we *are* to read into his character both the unattractive faults and the enduring strengths of traditional rural people. Yes, such a man is difficult to approach and understand, more difficult still to draw an empathetic response from us, so removed is he from the lives which we regard as desirable. Yet the strengths which our civilisation holds in high regard flourish because they have been grafted by generations on to the reliable root-stock of such as Iago Prytherch. Thomas implies that such a simple man is equipped to face even 'death's confusion'; his simplicity of purpose allows for no subtleties of metaphysics or theology.

The last ambiguity of the poem is in its final sentence. We should remember such a man as Iago 'for he, too, is a winner of wars'. What wars? How could a farmer win a war? Well, in the literal sense that British farmers, as R. S. Thomas must have been aware, fed the armies who would free Europe from Hitler. But there are two other senses: first, Iago's war is one of survival against the ravages of the elements in the mountains;

second, his peasant, or 'yeoman' stock traditionally provided the foot soldiers of European armies. The Welsh bowmen put paid to the French cavalry at Agincourt, while, in later wars, whether colonial or noble, Scots and Irish regiments proved themselves to be legendary fighters. Iago endures 'like a tree under the curious stars' – but is it the stars which remain curious, inexplicable symbols to the earth-bound farmer, or do the stars look down curiously on the pathos of his struggle to survive and advance. Again, I want to hold on to both possibilities, for I feel that such ambiguity is intriguingly at the core of the artist's purpose. Why settle for one meaning if you can achieve two in an image? There is a sense in which the poet is reminding us, the sophisticated readers of poetry, that we may be in no better position to read the significance of the stars than a peasant.

5   *Summarise my responses to the poem.*

A Peasant appears at first to be a poem centrally in the tradition of the English Romantics. Iago Prytherch is the sort of character to whom Wordsworth was drawn. The moral virtue of the rustic life and outlook is more dearly won in Thomas's poem, however, than in any of William Wordsworth's, for Thomas's hill farmer is revealed as a physically dirty and imaginatively bereft man, ground down by his life in the unyielding Welsh hills. R. S. Thomas makes us confront our natural repulsion in the face of such a character before imposing the nub of his argument, that Iago represents all our origins. He is the adamic root of all of us. Just as the poet has had to accept that fact, so too must we as we encounter the strength of his imagery.

Thomas has cleverly succeeded in drawing his reader into a position of false security, of distanced superiority, only to counter the bare facts of his 'peasant's' menial work and derelict appearance with a celebration of his rooted strength in labour on the land. From our position as voyeurs, tourists, we are drawn into an empathy from the recognition that it is a form of ourselves which we are being shown. Thomas's prosodic skill in creating the harsh details of this character's life now turns to address the positive virtues that have accrued to us all from that labouring heritage. At the end it is his strong back on which we depend, and who is to say that, at the distance of a star, his life is any the less significant than our own for that?

4

The 1960s

I noted in the previous chapter that the 1950s came to be characterised by some critics as the era dominated by the Group and the Movement. The 1960s was notable for the emergence and establishment of three major figures in post-war poetry – Ted Hughes, Sylvia Plath and Philip Larkin. Of these, only the last had been associated, and that loosely, with the poetry movements of the previous decade.

The 1960s were also notable for the attention which poetry generally attracted to itself in Britain, and this was due in no small part to the frequency and popularity of the poetry reading. In the 1950s in America we had been shown the possibility of large audiences for poets reading, or 'performing' their work. The 'Beat Poets' – Ginsberg, Ferlinghetti, Corso – together with the prose-poet/novelist Jack Kerouac, had offended convention by their language and behaviour and were to delight huge audiences through the Fifties and Sixties, often in ball-parks and football stadiums, with their combination of mysticism and outrage. In Britain, a number of poets had engaged with jazz musicians to stage performances; these included Dannie Abse and Vernon Scannell. My first enthusiasm for poetry other than that which I was encountering on the school textbook page, came from a record of Christopher Logue, with the Stan Tracey Quintet performing *Red Bird*, the love poems of Pablo Neruda in an intriguing combination of poetry and jazz. That version lifted poetry off the page and into an adolescent's imaginative concern. *Red Bird* was a poetry that sounded contemporary and vibrant.

In the late 1960s a slim Penguin paperback of poetry appeared which seemed to inject a fresh energy and enthusiasm into poetry as a directly experienced, contemporary form. Number 10 in the eclectic, affordable, immensely valuable series of *Penguin Modern Poets* was *The Mersey Sound*, which included selections from Adrian Henri, Roger McGough and Brian Patten. This was the first of that series to carry a title, and it is not difficult to see that, in 1967, 'The Mersey Sound' was a marketing ploy guaranteed to attract a new, younger audience to poetry. That audience had grown up with the Beatles, and with the fact of the serious newspaper critics reviewing pop albums alongside Beethoven, and Lennon and McCartney's poetic lyrics alongside those of Bob Dylan and W. H. Auden. Roger McGough became a notable 'cross-over' artist when he joined for a couple of years the pop group *Scaffold* and succeeded in the record charts. The three Mersey poets began a life of readings in pubs, colleges, clubs, on television and radio which was to continue a for a decade. While Adrian Henri has turned increasingly back to his work as a painter, McGough and Patten continue to produce books for children and collections of poetry. *The Mersey Sound* was reissued almost twenty years later in an enlarged version and has arguably been the best-selling book of contemporary poetry in Britain this century. It is likely that you will have come across one or more of these poets in school anthologies. It seems to me that they are often read in the context of 'enjoying poetry', though rarely used as formal study texts. There is, no doubt, a reason for that, but I shall have more to say about performance poetry and regional poetry later in this book. However, first I want to look at a poem by each of the major figures I mentioned at the start of this chapter – Larkin, Hughes and Plath. I'll start with a Philip Larkin poem which seems to me to be rooted in the Britain of the Fifties and early Sixties still in the process of emerging from a post-war trauma.

I

THE WHITSUN WEDDINGS
by Philip Larkin

That Whitsun, I was late getting away:
    Not till about
One-twenty on the sunlit Saturday
Did my three-quarters-empty train pull out,
All windows down, all cushions hot, all sense   5

Of being in a hurry gone. We ran
Behind the backs of houses, crossed a street
Of blinding windscreens, smelt the fish-dock; thence
The river's level drifting breadth began,
Where sky and Lincolnshire and water meet.   10

All afternoon, through the tall heat that slept
    For miles inland,
A slow and stopping curve southwards we kept.
Wide farms went by, short-shadowed cattle, and
Canals with floatings of industrial froth;   15
A hothouse flashed uniquely: hedges dipped
And rose: and now and then a smell of grass
Displaced the reek of buttoned carriage-cloth
Until the next town, new and nondescript,
Approached with acres of dismantled cars.   20

At first, I didn't notice what a noise
    The weddings made
Each station that we stopped at: sun destroys
The interest of what's happening in the shade,
And down the long cool platforms whoops and skirls   25
I took for porters larking with the mails,
And went on reading. Once we started, though,
We passed them, grinning and pomaded, girls
In parodies of fashion, heels and veils,
All posed irresolutely, watching us go,   30

As if out on the end of an event
    Waving goodbye
To something that survived it. Struck, I leant
More promptly out next time, more curiously,
And saw it all again in different terms: 35
The fathers with broad belts under their suits
And seamy foreheads; mothers loud and fat;
An uncle shouting smut; and then the perms,
The nylon gloves and jewellery-substitutes,
The lemons, mauves, and olive-ochres that   40

Marked off the girls unreally from the rest.
    Yes, from cafes
And banquet-halls up yards, and bunting-dressed

Coach-party annexes, the wedding-days
Were coming to an end. All down the line   45
Fresh couples climbed aboard: the rest stood round;
The last confetti and advice were thrown,
And, as we moved, each face seemed to define
Just what it saw departing: children frowned
At something dull; fathers had never known   50

Success so huge and wholly farcical;
       The women shared
The secret like a happy funeral;
While girls, gripping their handbags tighter, stared
At a religious wounding. Free at last,   55
And loaded with the sum of all they saw,
We hurried towards London, shuffling gouts of steam.
Now fields were building-plots, and poplars cast
Long shadows over major roads, and for
Some fifty minutes, that in time would seem   60

Just long enough to settle hats and say
       I nearly died,
A dozen marriages got under way.
They watched the landscape, sitting side by side
– An Odeon went past, a cooling tower,   65
And someone running up to bowl – and none
Thought of the others they would never meet
Or how their lives would all contain this hour.
I thought of London spread out in the sun,
Its postal districts packed like squares of wheat: 70

There we were aimed. And as we raced across
       Bright knots of rail
Past standing Pullmans, walls of blackened moss
Came close, and it was nearly done, this frail
Travelling coincidence; and what it held   75
Stood ready to be loosed with all the power
That being changed can give. We slowed again,
And as the tightened brakes took hold, there swelled
A sense of falling, like an arrow-shower
Sent out of sight, somewhere becoming rain.   80

1   *What sort of writing is shaped in front of me?*

This is a long poem divided into eight stanzas of ten lines. It is notable that the second line of each verse is indented and has no more than four words. Each line is marked, conventionally, with a capital letter. The verses, despite their length, nevertheless convey the reader with a run-on final line into the following verse. The majority of lines in the poem are run-on lines. The one instance of direct speech is italicised.

2   *Speak the poem to myself.*

This is quite a taxing poem: it is long, some 80 lines, and there are a number of long sentences that run-on through lines and from verse to verse. These long sentences are punctuated by commas, but also by an unusual number of semi-colons and colons. The pace and narrative direction are therefore a challenge, but the diction is not difficult and the sense of a humorous, wry personality behind the poem is immediately rewarding. There is a strong sense of being impelled by the narrative nature of the poem, and the range of characters who appear sustains the reader's interest.

At this early stage, I am conscious of the need to hear the sort of voice which is delivering this experience and commenting on the world he(?) is observing through the carriage window. My feeling is that if I can locate the exact tone of voice in this poem, then I will have gone a long way to understanding its effect and point of view.

3   *What patterns can I see in the poem?*

The overriding impression is that *The Whitsun Weddings* is a narrative that traces the writer's train journey from somewhere in the north of England down to London. The poem opens with a sense of rush, of discomfort and the unattractive inner city landscape that characterises the beginning of many British train journeys. The mood becomes more relaxed and rural between the various towns encountered on the journey. At its ending the poem mixes feelings of urban order and closure with what at first seems to be a strangely inappropriate image of movement and escape. However, the whole is held together by a tightly disciplined rhyme scheme that follows the pattern:

abab   cde   cde

Because the forward momentum of the narrative is so strong it may be that a third or fourth reading of the poem is needed before the full effect of the rhyme is grasped. Philip Larkin has obviously invested a lot of effort in his desire to counterpoint the narrative power of his poem with its run-on lines, by his weaving of rhymes which are, in the main, masculine, as, for example, 'ran' and 'began'. In each verse, too, the *abab* rhymes are undercut by the more distanced and less obvious *cdecde* rhymes which have the effect of propelling the verse to its conclusion, or into the next verse-paragraph.

The short second line in each verse has the effect of disjointing the verse. It is as if the narrator's feelings or thoughts hesitate for a moment. He seems to be working towards the words which best convey the experience of the journey and the sometimes strange, even alien sights which he is witnessing. These short lines break up the flow of the verse as the crossing of the railway points breaks the rhythm of a train's progress.

Of the eight verses, broadly speaking, the opening two set in motion the journey and establish the narrator's viewpoint. The middle four verses deal specifically with the weddings, and the last two verses describe the last leg of the journey, the train now packed with its cargo of new lives completing the run down to London.

4   *Discuss any ambiguities or paradoxes in the poem.*

As I have already mentioned, it seems that the key to this poem is the reader's grasp of the narrator-poet's tone of voice, his attitude towards the scenes which he is witnessing through his carriage-window. It would seem that in such a position he would be merely a passive receptor of whatever scenes and glimpsed relationships might happen to be framed by his window. It is at times as if he were an audience of one witnessing a kaleidoscopic series of performances. And yet his is just *one* vision, he occupies *one* seat on a rapidly filling passenger train. None of the events 'on the sunlit Saturday' is happening *to* the narrator (there is no reason to suppose this to be anyone other than Philip Larkin himself). Rather, Larkin sees himself to be outside the events, dispassionate, wry, a voyeur even. He is drawn briefly into one of the important moments in the lives of other people and yet because of the number of weddings (Whitsun being traditionally a popular weekend for betrothed couples) he is, paradoxically, detached from the individuality of the event. It is as if, in the middle four verses particularly, he is noting the rite of passage of a tribe previously unknown to him. He has the detachment of one of the 'mass observers' sent out to study the working-class 'tribes' of England in the 1930s. This coolness may strike the reader as unreasonably distancing the poet from what is after all a natural occurrence. It may be that some readers will detect an unpleasant, snobbishness in the tone of disapproval in the details of the wedding behaviour and 'paradies of fashion' –

> The nylon gloves and jewellery-substitutes,
> The lemons, mauves, and olive-ochres . . .
> And banquet-halls up yards, and bunting-dressed
> Coach-party annexes . . .

The middle verses work to undercut the validity of the weddings as uncomplicated means of dealing with life. Larkin, an outsider, sees the whole procedure for the elaborate social and sexual exercise that it is. By distinguishing the elements of the whole – the fathers' 'seamy foreheads', 'An uncle shouting smut', 'mothers loud and fat' – he is, essentially, questioning, even deconstructing the notion of the wedding day; perhaps of marriage itself. One may wonder whether the poet is writing from the viewpoint of an unfortunate experience of marriage himself, or whether he is a bachelor, inexperienced and averse to the institution. In the fourth verse, the lines –

> . . . Struck, I leant
> More promptly out next time, more curiously,
> And saw it all again in different terms:

indicate that Larkin is genuinely intrigued by the successive of wedding parties and the fact that he is forced to observe and question this particular rite for perhaps the first time. The journey throws at him a succession of instances, variations on the same theme, so that he is afforded the opportunity to analyse the elements which all these weddings have in common.

However, that explanation does not take account of the lingering sense that the poet is disapproving. A line such as

The fathers with broad belts under their suits

has a representative force which could be taken as a distortion. Are all fathers working-class? Does every suit hang unconvincingly on the frame, hitched crudely to a bulging stomach? Are all mothers loud and fat? Is there no silk, no wool, but only the poor taste of the poor – man-made nylons in man-made colours beneath dyed and permed hair? There is certainly a sense of caricature in the presentation of these people. We see them, through Larkin's eyes, as figures who could have stepped out of a cartoon; each incident, each set of characters is framed almost as a strip cartoon as the train unreels its evidence.

If that were the overriding and central impression which this poem made, then we might well be justified in dismissing the piece as prejudiced, 'standoffish', patronising in a dated way. We might take exception to this example of the poet as a rather remote, aloof observer of the lower orders and their rituals, (indeed, there are those who would want to stress the detached 'Englishness' of Larkin). However, my reading of *The Whitsun Weddings* is one which sees a more complex, subtler intention in the writing. I think that we would do well to return to the beginning of the poem to remind ourselves of the way in which the poet weaves together images of banality, of urban enclosure and images of the reluctant pastoral.

The poem opens conversationally; it is as if Larkin were beginning an anecdote, or an after dinner remembrance. It is only at 'thence', in line 8, that the underlying literariness of the writing is clearly signalled. It is an archaic word, with Romantic associations which contrast sharply with the banality of the journey's opening as the train steams away through the city's back streets. As the two concluding lines of the first verse follow 'thence' by connecting their rhymes with the previous *cde* endings, we get a sense of an opening out, an escape. However, our expectations of a developing pastoral are at first spoiled by 'floatings of industrial froth', and then displaced by 'acres of dismantled cars' at the edge of the 'next town, new and nondescript'. The 'short-shadowed cattle' and hothouse which 'flashed uniquely' are painterly reminders that this is indeed a fine Whitsun Saturday, but the reader has to share with the poet the ambiguous 'smell' and 'reek' respectively of grass and the carriage's upholstery. The effect of these opening verses is to establish Larkin as a meticulous, apparently detached observer of life. This means that when we encounter the more colourful (and *coloured*) impressions of the wedding parties that we are reluctant to question the stance of the narrator. He seems to be benefiting from the safe distance at which he feels to be removed from the events and feelings of the wedding couples, parents and guests.

In its final third the poem moves on into late afternoon, when 'poplars cast / Long shadows' and closer to the capital city's 'major roads'. Larkin assumes that none of the couples will meet or consider 'how their lives would all contain this hour'. Then comes a rather strange sentence, an apparent *non sequitur* −

> I thought of London spread out in the sun,
> Its postal districts packed with squares of wheat:
>
> There we were aimed.

Making the connection between those two observations is, I think, the key to Larkin's poem. He has brought together the human (perhaps for him all-too-human) rite, interwoven by circumstance, with the sense of seasonal fertility. The administrational ploy of dividing a great city into postal areas, incidentally, creates the impression of an aerial view of fields, as in some feudal plan. People settle and grow in those areas; the buildings and communities there are the fruits of our civilisation. And all of that life is founded on the procreation of human beings, the focus of which in our society is the institution of marriage. Though Philip Larkin seems, both by circumstance and by disposition, to be removed from that activity, and though he can see the ceremony for the complex of social, emotional and behavioural confusions and fumblings that it always seems to be, the one thing that his journey leads him to is the realisation that this is the way that life progresses. His acknowledgement of that fact transforms the significance of the train journey. He ends the poem by describing the event in terms much more metaphorical than he or his reader might have predicted. Now he wants to describe 'all the power / That being changed can give'. Life, after all, is about movement and change; it is a journey, a progression, albeit along the tracks which society has laid down, and dressed in the manner which custom decrees.

The final sentence of the poem develops and, I would argue, resolves the ambiguity of the journey. The 'tightened brakes' should convey a sense of arrival, safety, conclusion: instead, there is 'A sense of falling' that removes any feeling of purpose or intention. There is a passivity, like that of an arrow powered and directed by another hand and eye, but then curving in its trajectory beyond that original intent. 'Sent out of sight', the train and its passengers are seen to be 'like an arrow-shower . . . somewhere becoming rain'. How can a shower of arrows become rain? Well, Larkin is turning the original metaphor back on itself: might not a shower of arrows – weapons of death after all – become positive, refreshing rain out of sight of their archer and beyond his original intention? The lives of the passengers are like a sheaf of arrows directed from their various stations and backgrounds, but flying with the possibility of quite different targets and an unlimited power to affect change in themselves and the society which has produced them.

5   *Summarise my responses to the poem.*

The *Whitsun Weddings* is an intriguing poem which addresses something elemental and central in all our lives. It at first invites by its conversational tone, then draws us along a journey which becomes more complex and varied as station after station imposes wedding scenes, marriages which are loaded onto the train and which then progress together towards a destination. This destination is, literally, London, but a London transformed into a sort of harvest field of growth and fruition. The whole experience is perceived, and coloured, by the persona of Larkin himself, and the effect which it has on us is qualified by our response to the sort of character that we consider Larkin to be. We engage in the nature of the experience as it deepens in significance for him. His description of the wedding parties is witty and, no matter how reluctant we may be to accept the implicit judgements he seems to be making about these people, the poet may be seen to redeem himself and them by his concluding metaphor. The poem's conclusion rises above and beyond the physical train journey to celebrate the possibilities of renewal and growth. T. S. Eliot in his poem *The Wasteland* leant heavily on traditional (and obscure) fertility myths in order to deal with the despair and desolation of post First World War Europe and his own personal, emotional problems. Philip Larkin, by involving us in the rites of passage of ordinary lives, succeeds in creating a mythical dimension in *The Whitsun Weddings* that is at once rooted in the familiar and transcending it.

II

THRUSHES
by Ted Hughes

Terrifying are the attent sleek thrushes on the lawn,
More coiled steel than living – a poised
Dark deadly eye, those delicate legs
Triggered to stirrings beyond sense – with a start,
                              a bounce, a stab
Overtake the instant and drag out some writhing thing.
No indolent procrastinations and no yawning stares.
No sighs or head-scratchings. Nothing but bounce
                              and stab
And a ravening second.

Is it their single-minded-sized skulls, or a trained
Body, or genius, or a nestful of brats
Gives their days this bullet and automatic
Purpose? Mozart's brain had it, and the shark's mouth
That hungers down the blood-smell even to a leak
                              of its own
Side and devouring of itself: efficiency which
Strikes too streamlined for any doubt to pluck at it
Or obstruction deflect.

With a man it is otherwise. Heroisms on horseback,
Outstripping his desk-diary at a broad desk,
Carving at a tiny ivory ornament
For years: his act worships itself – while for him,
Though he bends to be blent in the prayer, how
                              loud and above what
Furious spaces of fire do the distracting devils
Orgy and hosannah, under what wilderness
Of black silent waters weep.

1   *What sort of writing is shaped in front of me?*

This is a poem of twenty-four lines arranged in three stanzas
of eight lines. It follows the convention of capital letters at the
beginning of each line, though there is no immediate sense of
regular line-lengths which would suggest a metrical pattern. In
fact, there is a considerable disparity between lines as short as the
eighth and, say, the twenty-first. The poem also seems irregular
because the poet has used three dashes to interrupt lines. On
closer examination I find that in each verse the second and third
lines are shorter than the others, and that the concluding line of
each verse is the shortest in each verse. It is as if each verse were
coming to an abrupt climax.

2   *Speak the poem to myself.*

This is not a particularly easy or straightforward poem to read.
Some sentences are quite complex, and there are a number of
words which seem unfamiliar – 'attent', 'ravening' 'blent' and
'hosannah' (used as a verb, I think). I can now hear the effect
of those dashes. The first puts into parenthesis the detail of
description regarding the thrushes which the poet has seen
(is seeing?) on the lawn. In the third verse, however, the dash
signals the conclusion of the poem (and the argument?) and sets
a sort of cosmic view of 'a man' against the detailed activities to
which, and through which, we dedicate our lives.
   There are eight sentences in the poem. The first and last
of these are quite challenging, for they are complicated in their
syntax and carry the burden of the poem. It is held in the tension
between these two poles: the nature of the thrushes' unthinking
response to their desire for food, the triggering of the action by
a sudden movement of their prey, and then the contrasting complexities of the human psyche, with its more varied dedications
to action and its overwhelming awareness of a wider context. But
neither one is uncomplicated in the way that Ted Hughes presents
it; the treatment of the thrushes' apparently direct action brings
in comparisons with other creatures, and the third verse sets out
to indicate the complexities which surround Mankind.
   What one can say, after two or three further readings, is that the
language benefits from patternings of sounds. There is alliteration
– 'Dark deadly' 'Strikes too streamlined' 'Heroisms on horseback'

and 'wilderness . . . waters weep'. There is assonance – 'Bends to be blent', 'tiny ivory' – and the hint of internal consonant rhymes: 'Skulls / nestful', 'genius / purpose', 'bullet / had it'. Locating these is a way of confirming the sense you have when reading this poem of a richness of sounds and a depth of meaning. There may be no rhyming pattern in this poem, but there is a clear sense of purpose to the line lengths. Most effective in controlling pace and directing attention are the run-on lines 'poised / Dark deadly eye', 'delicate legs / Triggered to stirrings', 'which / Strikes too stream-lined' and the four final lines which, I think, exemplify the possi-bilities of free verse to elevate language above the limitations of prose. There will, clearly, be much more to say about the end of this poem, but it should be evident, already, that the effect is one of a heightened, almost biblical tone.

3   What patterns can I see in the poem?

Of course, the three verses of equal length form the basis for Ted Hughes's consideration of thrushes. I have noted that the line-lengths create a pattern of sorts. In the first two verses the opening sentence is a long one, while the opening of the final verse is abrupt and prepares us for the longest and most complex of statements, as befits humankind. The opening description is also detailed and complex, setting up the puzzlement of the poet and the reader, but he does not at this point enquire more deeply into the appearance of the birds on his lawn. The three short sentences that follow deny the possibility of human associations in the birds' actions. 'Indolent procrastinations', 'yawning stares' and 'head-scratchings' are only for humans and their elaborate idea of their own lives – Prince Hamlet, King Lear, Faustus.

The second verse explores further this bewildering simplicity of the birds' actions: Hughes proposes various behaviourist explanations, but seems convinced by not a single one of them. Humankind, however, is far more complicated, as we are reminded in the last verse. Not for us the single-minded act, the instant response. No, we are situated in the midst of contesting myths and beliefs. Through the three verses Hughes takes us to ourselves by way of a structured argument: first, consider thrushes, how they are distinct from us, not prey to the abstractions of humankind; secondly, what makes them that way, what is the cause and effect relationship in their world? Lastly, by comparison, are we humans not indulgent, trapped by our own imaginings, doomed by those very qualities which distinguish us from the other creatures?

The organisation of this poem and its argument into three equal parts helps to reinforce the impression of a reasonable consideration of the situation of humankind. But the distance our thoughts have travelled in this short poem is quite immense, so that, at the end, we may be forgiven for wondering how on earth we arrived at the cosmic fate of humanity when all we were doing was watching birds on the lawn. Enquiring into the nature of that paradox take us to our next question.

4   *Discuss any ambiguities or paradoxes in the poem.*

The title of the poem would appear to be quite straightforward. A poem about birds; ordinary birds which are common to our gardens. But immediately, with the first word, we are unsettled. 'Terrifying' is hardly the way we usually describe thrushes. Do we assume that the poet is in some way disturbed, neurotic? That possibility is dismissed rapidly as the fist verse establishes the perception and clarity of intelligence of the writer. It is as if he himself is sharpened by the example of the thrushes. His poem satisfies one of the basic expectations that we as readers have of the medium: there is an intensification of experience, an elevation of the banal. As Norman MacCaig, that fine Scottish poet has said, the poem has rendered 'the ordinary extraordinary'. Perhaps that is one of the most compelling justifications for the writing of poetry; if we can be encouraged to perceive details from our everyday life in a heightened way, acknowledging the uniqueness of everything, then our living will have been enriched. That is the motivation of the poets our culture holds in esteem such as Shakespeare, Blake and Wordsworth and it is what draws readers to outstanding contemporary poets like Ted Hughes. There is something incisive and even predatory about the poet's approach. That first line with its stabbing 't' sounds and its foreshortening of 'attentive' to 'attent' is paradoxically dramatical. The verse continues to subvert our conventional ideas of thrushes with descriptions such as 'Dark deadly', 'coiled steel' and 'Triggered'. These birds are aggressive and furious in their urge to eat and survive. And yet they have 'delicate legs' and a 'sleek' coat. These light birds are, in their own terms, remarkably destructive and decisive. They 'overtake the instant' and are startlingly direct in their consumption of 'some writhing thing' in 'a ravening second'. Hughes is deliberately shocking us out of our bland assumptions regarding the birds, and regarding the whole of the natural world which pursues its life around us. Birds, at a safe distance, through our windows, in the trees in our gardens, are decorative and we indulge them. But the fact of their lives is as basic as that of all natural things: they sing to court and warn; they fly for food and safety; they land and peck to search and kill their food. The poet reminds us that the name for a raven incorporates the sense of a rapacious, gluttonous assault. A bird may represent not only delicacy and beauty, but the underlying violence by which the world moves.

In the second verse Hughes lists the various possible motivations for the birds' actions. Could it be the very limitations of their brain power, or a set of learned behavioural responses, or the urge to feed their young? Or might it be 'genius'? This last is slotted into that list almost casually, but is the nub of the argument. 'Genius' is a catch-all word for those exemplary qualities which we recognise in other human beings whom we call unique. Building on that list, Hughes makes his point further by the odd comparison of Mozart and a shark's unthinking voraciousness 'even to a leak of its own / Side and devouring of itself'. He then goes even further in claiming that this represents a sort of 'efficiency'. The imagery throughout this verse is very interesting. The reader is not allowed to settle into any reassuring assumptions about language. One is no more likely to have thought of Mozart's compositions as resulting from 'bullet and automatic / Purpose' than to have recognised 'genius' in the life of a thrush.

In the final verse 'a man' presumably stands for those of us who do not aspire to Mozart's genius. For the rest of us, mere mortals by comparison, it is 'Heroisms on horseback' (in fact, or by association in our fictions and films) or the petty achievements of desk-bound bureaucracy, or the obsessional small-scale expression of a carved object by which we must rise above the banal facts of living. Paradoxically, it seems that this range of activities pales beside the 'triggered' purity of action of the thrush. Though we wish to be involved totally, 'to be blent' in our prayers (I take this to mean 'blend into' the purity of our wishes), we are doomed by the very power of our imaginations. Above us, constantly, our concepts of hell and heaven contest. All our lives we are distracted from the instant of action by a cosmic superstructure of eternal significance, the moral consequences of those actions. Our imagination traps us into fears, so that we ourselves become the prize of contesting Good and Evil.

The language of the final five lines of the poem itself compounds the point Hughes wishes to make. The syntax of the second part of that sentence is complex and grandiose. It is as if he is dismissing the possibility of our emulating the birds' simplicity by the very act of articulating the problem. Language is our means of objectifying and therefore rationalising the facts of our experience and the compulsion of our feelings. It is, however, also the chain that binds us to what we see as the consequences of our actions. This means that the greatest paradox is that the poem itself is the very antithesis of direct action. *Thrushes* has twisted and tricked the reader in much the same way as Shakespeare's 'Shall I compare Thee to a Summer's day?' in Chapter 1.

5   *Summarise my responses to the poem.*

This is a difficult poem which requires several readings. However, the demands which it makes on us are justified because, it can be argued, they are at the core of the poem's meaning anyway. What is reassuringly conventional about the poem is its strategy of moving on and out from an ordinary observation to a more profound consideration of life's issues. That is the sort of development we have been conditioned to expect from literary texts and other works of art, from the still life to the opera. Hughes, from the very first word of his poem, works to elevate and extend our response to thrushes as examples of those life-forms around us of which we may usually take little interest. In a way, he is both developing and subverting the famous lines of William Blake:

> How do you know but that every bird that cuts the
>   aery way
> Is an immense world of delight, clos'd by your
>   senses five?

Well, how do you know? says Hughes. Because you don't consider the meaning and consequences of direct action, untrammelled by the indulgence of your imagination and the need humans have for the theological dimension, you don't recognise that genius is based on a simplicity that is, in a sense, callous and unwavering, 'a stab/ (to) Overtake the instant'. We are, because of our superior intelligence, self-reflective beings, our act 'worships itself', rather than working 'too streamlined for any doubt'. We are, his poem argues, victims of our own advancement. Our prayers and poems are both the symptom of our condition and, paradoxically, one of the ways in which we deal with the dilemma.

III

DADDY
by Sylvia Plath

You do not do, you do not do
Any more, black shoe
In which I have lived like a foot
For thirty years, poor and white,
Barely daring to breathe or Achoo.

Daddy, I have had to kill you.
You died before I had time –
Marble-heavy, a bag full of God,
Ghastly statue with one grey toe
Big as a Frisco seal

And a head in the freakish Atlantic
Where it pours bean green over blue
In the waters off beautiful Nauset.
I used to pray to recover you.
Ach, du.

In the German tongue, in the Polish town
Scraped flat by the roller
Of wars, wars, wars.
But the name of the town is common.
My Polack friend

Says there are a dozen or two.
So I never could tell where you
Put your foot, your root,
I never could talk to you.
The tongue stuck in my jaw.

It stuck in a barb wire snare.
Ich, ich, ich, ich,
I could hardly speak.
I thought every German was you.
And the language obscene

An engine, an engine
Chuffing me off like a Jew.
A Jew to Dachau, Auschwitz, Belsen.
I began to talk like a Jew.
I think I may well be a Jew.

The snows of the Tyrol, the clear beer of Vienna
Are not very pure or true.
With my gypsy ancestress and my weird luck
And my Taroc pack and my Taroc pack
I may be a bit of a Jew.

I have always been scared of *you*,
With your Luftwaffe, your gobbledygoo.
And your neat moustache
And your Aryan eye, bright blue.
Panzer-man, panzer-man, O you –

Not God but a swastika
So black no sky could squeak through.
Every woman adores a Fascist,
The boot in the face, the brute
Brute heart of a brute like you.

You stand at the blackboard, daddy,
In the picture I have of you,
A cleft in your chin instead of your foot
But no less a devil for that, no not
Any less the black man who

Bit my pretty red heart in two.
I was ten when they buried you.

At twenty I tried to die
And get back, back, back to you.
I thought even the bones would do.

But they pulled me out of the sack,
And they stuck me together with glue.
And then I knew what to do.
I made a model of you,
A man with a Meinkampf look

And a love of the rack and screw.
And I said I do, I do.
So, daddy, I'm finally through.
The black telephone's off at the root,
The voices just can't worm through.

If I've killed one man, I've killed two —
The vampire who said he was you
And drank my blood for a year,
Seven years, if you want to know.
Daddy, you can lie back now.

There's a stake in your fat black heart
And the villagers never liked you.
They are dancing and stamping on you.
They always *knew* it was you.
Daddy, daddy, you bastard, I'm through.

1   *What sort of writing is shaped in front of me?*

Daddy is a long poem comprising sixteen verses, each of five
lines. The lines never appear to settle into a regularity of length
and what I perceive to be essentially a short line can, at times,
be stretched —

> The snows of the Tyrol, the clear beer of Vienna

and at other times cut short in an almost peremptory way —

> Ach, du.

Perhaps this is not so surprising, for a poem of some 80
lines in regular verse lengths needs to be varied in pace.

2   *Speak the poem to myself.*

This proves to be both a strange and remarkable experience. The lines flow with a rhythmic force that is punctuated primarily by the frequent occurrence of the word 'you' and other words which rhyme with it. This sense of rhythm is built up by the stress of, usually, three or four syllables in each line, through the repetition of syntax, the parallelism which occurs time and time again:

> With my gypsy ancestress and my weird luck
> And my Taroc pack and my Taroc pack

In fact, there is a strong sense of the incantatory chant about this poem; one is forced to persist with that accusatory tone. Certainly the strange and perplexing shifts of reference and focus – a black shoe, the poet's father, a Jew of the Holocaust, a fortune-teller, a vampire – are held together in a very necessary way by the sound of the poem. It is that which goes a long way towards reassuring the reader, who might otherwise become exasperated by the demands of the poem's imagery. If we are drawn back to *Daddy* in a renewed attempt to appreciate its purpose, then it is the bewitching(?) 'sound' of the poem which holds us. The 'you' sound makes us purse our lips continually, as if whistling up a spectre. Then, by contrast, there is a deliberate ugliness, a grating of gutteral sounds –

> It stuck in a barb wire snare.
> Ich, ich, ich, ich,

in verse 6 and in the litany of Nazi death-camps in verse 7 which is quite appropriate to the nature of such horrors.

I have mentioned the persistent rhyming of 'you', but most of the other lines rhyme, though some of them are imperfect rhymes. There are consonant rhymes – 'foot/ white', 'obscene/ engine', 'sack/ look', and internal rhymes – 'you/ statue', 'foot/ root', 'boot/ brute', 'sack/ stuck'. This device is particularly important in the stressed '*knew*' and 'you' of the final verse.

There is, too, much use made of assonance – 'Barely, daring', 'Ghastly statue', 'Tongue stuck' and the chilling 'Dachau, Auschwitz'. The whole poem weaves together combinations of sounds and tricks of language so that the effect becomes one of an almost obsessional nature. It seems that Plath cannot articulate without drawing attention to the artifice of language. That observation should take us on to our next point of enquiry.

3   What patterns can I see in the poem?

The patterning of sound in this poem has already been made clear in the valuable process of reading the piece aloud. The regularity of verse length has also been pointed out, as has the tendency to stress either three or four syllables per line. The rhyming of words at line-endings or internally does not, however, appear to follow any set pattern. It is important to note that almost every line is linked by one or more rhymes or repetitions and that this persistence of rhyme is strengthened as we go further into the poem. The effect is that of intensifying the insistence and strength of the poet's voice. As we have noted previously, the patterning of language in poetry, as in oratory – sermons and speeches – works to convince the reader or listener of the implicit worth of the argument propounded. That conviction in the rightness of the poet's stance in *Daddy* will be seriously tested by the extremes of emotion which the poem generates. To come to terms with the power of the poem as a whole we will have to move on to ask our next question.

4   Discuss any ambiguities or paradoxes in the poem.

Again, it is with the title that our first puzzlement comes. *Daddy* is, of course, a term of endearment, yet the first verse seems, initially, to be strangely irrelevant, and with the first line of the second verse, 'Daddy, I have had to kill you.', the poet has completely overturned our expectations. What we must do, then, is to build positively on what we can regard as firm at the beginning of this poem. As with the Dylan Thomas poem in Chapter 3, we must always return to the premise that the poet does indeed intend these lines and images and that they are aware that their readers will be made to work in order to reach the point of the poem. The efforts which we as readers make in order to decode the literary text must be essential to the poet's intention, and *must* be, ultimately, rewarding for us. Works of art are their forms, their shapes and the demands they make; otherwise we might as well settle for slogans and soap opera. If Sylvia Plath opens her poem in a strangely oblique way, then might that not be because the subject of her poem and the emotions which that raises for her are difficult and painful?

What we can be sure of is that the poet / persona of the poem is thirty, white, female. The 'black shoe' reminds one of 'The Woman Who Lived In A Shoe' from the nursery rhyme. There's no mention of a hoard of children in the poem, but there is certainly a sense of constriction, of being forced into a set of circumstances which she can no longer tolerate. The whole tone of the poem is that of witty and sarcastic protest and violent responses to such constraints. Surely the idea that each generation has partly to destroy the previous generation, 'a bag full of God', in order to assert and express itself is as old as Greek poetry and theatre. What is unusual in this poem is the sense of disappointment that her 'Daddy' died before she could 'kill' him. Like all parents, Sylvia Plath's father seems, in memory, larger than life, 'Ghastly statue with one grey toe / Big as a Frisco seal', and yet, at awful moments, vulnerable, susceptible to drowning: notice how Plath creates a child's fear of losing their parents in some world-wide ocean of their nightmares –

> In the waters off beautiful Nauset,
> I used to pray to recover you.

The following rhyme, 'Ach, du', is clearly German, and though I don't speak that language I think that it means 'Ah, so,' or 'Oh, you'. In any case, the main purpose of that short, gutteral line is to link up with the following images of central Europe in the Second World War. The shifting and threatened identities of peoples in those regions was and is a central issue in this century, from the Treaty of Versailles to the Cold War which was chilling international relations through the 1950s and at the time this poem was written. However, these images, particularly those which are built out of the references to the Nazi genocide of the Jews, are the most dramatic and perplexing of this poem.

Sylvia Plath is obviously an American: her sea is the Atlantic, off the eastern seaboard of the USA; she uses the slang (and somewhat derogatory) 'Polack' instead of Polish; her seal is as large as a 'Frisco' seal. Yet she is clearly disturbed by the fact that her father is somehow implicated in the collective guilt of a Germany publicly castigated following the Second World War. The terrible burden of holocaust memories is so heavy for the poet that she imagines herself a Jew. Certainly, the central verses of this poem are both disturbing in their emotive references, and confusing in their shifting of focus. Are we to take it that Sylvia Plath's father actually *was* a Nazi party member, with his 'Meinkampf look', his 'Luftwaffe' and his 'Aryan eye'? He is called 'Panzer-man, panzer-man' and is seen to dominate her life like some immense statue.

> Not God but a swastika
> So black no sky could squeak through.

Furthermore, she goes on to claim that 'Every woman adores a Fascist', but that is surely tongue-in-cheek, for haven't we been alerted to the fact that Sylvia Plath, for whatever reason, has not constructed this poem in a completely logical, linear manner?

If we look back at verses 6, 7 and 8 we can see that she progresses from the sound of the German 'ich' to the suggestion of barbed wire and then to the death-camps. Verse 8 moves from picture postcard images of the Austro-German culture to a mysterious suggestion of fortune-telling, gypsy ancestry. The progress is, then, by a sort of imaginative improvisation. Maybe the key to this poem lies in its exaggerated fears, the complex of fantasy and ignorance which the poet has with regard to her father. She seems often to be swept from image to image principally by the sound of the words. For example, 'your gobbledygoo', and the echo of 'boot' in 'the brute / Brute heart of a brute like you'. The effect may be said to be that of a wild, angered confusion funnelled through the tight spiralling of these short, rhymed verses.

We learn in verse 11 that 'Daddy' was a teacher, but no sooner is that image of (comparative) normality presented, than the poem introduces the comparison of Sylvia Plath's father as some sort of 'devil', a 'vampire' who 'Bit my pretty red heart in two' who 'drank my blood for a year' and who is ritually killed by the villagers who, in any case, 'never liked you'. At this point we must recognise that Sylvia Plath's poem is entirely unconventional; though she calls on a range of conventions – the villainy of war, the sorcery of gypsies, the vampire myths of mid-European folk tales – as a means of giving expression to the complexity of feelings which her father arouses. The key to the poem must therefore lie in the realisation that Plath is prepared to stretch our credulity in order to express her feelings. She has plucked imagery out of the air, out of her life's history and her reading, to relate to her emotions. In this way she generates a quite bewildering and original energy through her range of images. And all of this derives from a love / hate relationship with her father.

But it is not as simple as that, is it? There is one further ambiguity to think about before we can feel confident in our responses to this poem. We have learnt that Sylvia Plath was ten when her father died. At twenty, she says, she 'tried to die / And get back, back, back to you'. If this was indeed a suicide attempt then it was obviously unsuccessful, but the poet seems to be indicating that she was left in a still fragile state: 'they stuck me together with glue.' Then, most strangely, paradoxically of all,

> I made a model of you
> A man with a Meinkampf look
>
> And a love of the rack and screw.

If this is someone other than her father, then there are two people contained in the figure of 'Daddy'. The next line surely provides us with a solution to this confusing situation.

> And I said I do, I do.

Those are the words spoken at the altar in the marriage ceremony. The man who had dominated her early life is finally, irrevocably divorced from the poet. Her father has left a gap in her life which has now been filled by her husband. That is the conventional wisdom of the marriage act in our society. It is one of the rites of passage which Philip Larkin realised as he witnessed the wedding parties on station after station that Whitsun Saturday. If her wedding represented the possibility of a new start for her, then it is immediately soured by the harshness of

> The black telephone's off at the root,
> The voices just can't worm through.

While that consigns her father to a coffined oblivion, the next verse loads a double burden of guilt upon the poet:

If I've killed one man, I've killed two –

The implication is that her marriage, 'Seven years, if you want to know' was a debilitating blood-letting; the experience has drained her vitality as surely as a vampire in a horror film. There the Dracula figure is a male parasite who preys on female victims. It is one of the most disturbing (and, apparently, compulsive) metaphors in our European mythology of monsters and fears.

Sylvia Plath's poem can be seen as a chant, a surreal litany which works to exorcise her life of the men she feels she has suffered by. If the final image is bizarre, a horror film escapism, then it is also a defiant and possibly triumphant escape.

5 *Summarise my responses to the poem.*

This is a mesmerising, but disturbing poem in which Sylvia Plath addresses her father and, through him, her idea of men. It is not a complimentary portrayal, for the images which she feels most apposite to her feelings are some of the most terrible of the twentieth century. Her father is, we are told, a German-speaker, probably an immigrant to the USA. Sylvia Plath's relationship with him has been a complex of suspicion, distaste and guilt. She has found it difficult to relate to him, 'The tongue stuck in my jaw', and has fantasised his death and attempted to take her own life. Whether this has been caused by her despair at her unhappy childhood, or whether she has become severely depressed because of the horrors of the times in which she has lived, we may not be sure. Certainly, the form of the poem, its sharp, short verses and, especially, its insistence on the 'you' rhyme creates a witty but obsessional effect. The poem is redeemed from the charge of self-indulgence by the honesty which she applies to her own weaknesses and her continuing sense of confusion regarding her true nature. What is clear is that, at the poem's end, Plath can assert a stubborn, hard-won strength. She proclaims her determination to strike out for her own needs. I think that the level of honesty will impress many readers and that they will appreciate the fact that Sylvia Plath's problems with her father are not unique, even if her choice of imagery is quite unusual.

I should not be surprised if many people, particularly perhaps women, responded strongly to this poem and empathised with the poet. The extension of the 'Daddy' figure, so that it encompasses Sylvia Plath's husband too, proposes an explanation of the way women and men relate that is surely 'feminist'. Having said that, I would not want to give the impression that this poem is merely sloganising; like all the best political writings, it has wit and originality. This poem aims to undermine the assumptions of readers regarding the conventional subject matter of poetry, and the way in which Plath maintains a tension between painful revelation, chilling historical reference and witty, almost vaudeville humour is both entertaining and subversive.

5

The 1970s

In this chapter I want to look at three poems by poets who had established reputations before the 1970s, but whose work reached a maturity during that decade which confirmed them as distinctive voices. I have chosen a poem by Seamus Heaney which was first published in the 1960s and included in his *Selected Poems 1965-1975*. *Death of a Naturalist* was the title poem of his first book, published in 1966, and was very widely anthologised through the 1970s. It has become one of the 'set pieces' for teachers and examiners as an 'unseen poem' for practical criticism. I have also chosen poems by Dannie Abse and Leslie Norris who are two of our most accomplished poets and writers of fiction. Both men had written from their early twenties, but their best work began to appear in the 1970s. All three writers have a body of work which has rested heavily on autobiography, the detailed description of actual places and events, but which is also capable of surprising, at times, surreal effects.

I

DEATH OF A NATURALIST
by Seamus Heaney

All year the flax-dam festered in the heart
Of the townland; green and heavy headed
Flax had rotted there, weighted down by huge sods.
Daily it sweltered in the punishing sun.
Bubbles gargled delicately, bluebottles
Wove a strong gauze of sound around the smell.
There were dragon-flies, spotted butterflies,
But best of all was the warm thick slobber
Of frogspawn that grew like clotted water

In the shade of the banks. Here, every spring
I would fill jampotfuls of the jellied
Specks to range on window-sills at home,
On shelves at school, and wait and watch until
The fattening dots burst into nimble-
Swimming tadpoles. Miss Walls would tell us how
The daddy frog was called a bull frog
And how he croaked and how the mammy frog
Laid hundreds of little eggs and this was
Frogspawn. You could tell the weather by frogs too
For they were yellow in the sun and brown
In rain.

Then one day when fields were rank
With cowdung in the grass the angry frogs
Invaded the flax-dam; I ducked through hedges
To a coarse croaking that I had not heard
Before. The air was thick with a bass chorus.
Right down the dam gross-bellied frogs were cocked
On sods; their loose necks pulsed like sails. Some hopped:
The slap and plop were obscene threats. Some sat
Poised like mud grenades, their blunt heads farting.
I sickened, turned and ran. The great slime kings
Were gathered for vengeance and I knew
That if I dipped my hand the spawn would clutch it.

1   *What sort of writing is shaped in front of me?*

This is a poem of 33 lines, divided into 2 sections of 21 and 12 lines
respectively. Although the left margins are justified and the capital letter convention is followed, the second section begins with
the sort of indentation we associate with a paragraph of prose. The
lines appear to be fairly uniform in length, with the exception of
the final line of the first section which is the abrupt 'In rain'.

2   *Speak the poem to myself.*

This is a comparatively straightforward poem to read. There
is no difficulty in understanding any of the words, though I
am certainly aware that the poet has combined sounds in an

interesting way. The image in lines 8 and 10 is particularly striking in its evocation of a tactile experience; there is a special (almost wicked) pleasure in speaking,

> But best of all was the warm thick slobber
> Of frogspawn that grew like clotted water
> In the shade of the banks.

That choice of 'slobber' cleverly combines a child's delight in body fluids with a derogatory noun. There are many instances of assonance and alliteration. The narrative element in this poem carries the reader steadily through to an ending which will, clearly, require further thought. The first section seems to present a scene familiar to childhood learning, both natural and in the controlled context of the classroom; while the second section seems further on in time and more grown-up in its language and vision. The 'obscene threats' and 'their blunt heads farting' immediately strike me as somewhat shocking.

3   *What patterns can I see in the poem?*

I have already mentioned the narrative strength of this poem and, in the absence of any rhyme scheme or regularity of rhythm, it is the pacing of this narrative and the qualities of sound and imagery which draw the reader back into the poem. The most important organising principle to discuss is the division of the poem into two sections. I should point out that the first section introduces the landscape of the poem and, in an amusing way, describes the traditional role of the tadpole in junior schools. The second section picks up the tone of the poem's opening lines and confirms the darker aspects of the flax-dam. What had seemed hopeful, an instructive experience of life in microcosm, has turned into a disturbing confrontation with the ugliness of the 'gross-bellied frogs'. The 'nimble-/Swimming tadpoles' have become 'The great slime kings'; the hopeful promise of early life has become an aggressive confrontation with the adult 'angry frogs'.

Heaney breaks some of the lines in a balanced way. Sometimes the line is punctuated – 'Flax had rotted there, weighted down by huge sods.' At other times the line has a natural balance in its phrasing – 'But best of all was the warm thick slobber', where the pause seems to me to come naturally for effect after the word 'all'. Most lines run on to complete their clause or sentence in the following line. This is an effective way of progressing the narrative drive of the piece.

I have already mentioned the fact that this poem creates interesting patterns of sounds. I should give some examples of that. In the opening of the poem Heaney is determined to re-create the atmosphere of the flax-dam as vividly as he can. To that end he chooses, in the first ten lines, to load his images heavily with words that stretch vowels and insist on a certain weightiness in their consonants: the flax is 'green and heavy headed'; it had 'rotted there, weighted down by huge sods'. The 't' and 'd' sounds weigh the images and slow them down. He chooses 'weighted' rather than the more conventional 'weighed' for the same reason. The lines,

> Wove a strong gauze of sound around the smell.
> There were dragon-flies, spotted butterflies,

emphasise 's' and 'z' sounds which evoke the bluebottles and other winged creatures that fill the air above the dam. In the last twelve lines of the first section the alliteration, 'jampotfuls of the jellied', 'wait and watch', and the repetition of 'frog' help to create a sense of innocent wonderment; there is also the steady acquisition of knowledge through observation and repetitive stating of facts about 'The daddy frog' and 'the mammy frog'.

In the second section there is a darkening sense of the world as a threatening place: 'coarse croaking' greets his approach. 'Right down the dam gross-bellied frogs were cocked / On sods.' They 'hopped' with a 'slap and plop' so that the reader *hears* the bubbling mud that seems to lie in wait like a mouth for him; though it is the natural habitat for the grown frogs and distinguishes their existence from his and ours.

At three points in the poem, then, Heaney uses a concentration of sound effects to evoke firstly the tangible sense of an atmosphere, then, the innocence of the classroom and, finally, the ugliness of the world outside.

4   *Discuss any ambiguities or paradoxes in the poem.*

As we have often found, the poem's title is the first thing that requires consideration under this heading. *Death of a Naturalist* is a title which might lead us to expect a narrative that includes hazardous exploration, perhaps to a mountain in Scotland, or an exotic rain-forest; we might suppose that some tragedy is to befall the protagonist; he might fall, become frozen, or be attacked by a wild animal. Our naturalist is heroically to sacrifice himself in order to extend the frontiers of knowledge, in order to add to the sum of the human experience. What we are presented with by Heaney is an autobiographical memoir of his early days in school and the predictable gathering of tadpoles for the classroom tank. Our first reaction might well be to regard the title, then, as ironical, tongue-in-cheek. It is. However, the poem does, in its own terms, fulfil those other, grander expectations occasioned by its title, and we would be advised to follow them through in our critical reading of the text.

There is a sense of exploration at the beginning of the poem, albeit 'in the heart / Of the townland'. The heat and closeness of the atmosphere, 'a strong gauze of sound around the smell', suggests somewhere more exotic. Don't young children have a particular ability and need to fantasise such foreign landscapes in their games? The flax-dam has many of the qualities of the jungle, but the spoils of the expedition are transformed into the safe spectacle of the early stages of the tadpoles' life-cycle, ranged 'on window-sills at home, / On shelves in school'. But, of course, what happens in the jampots and school fish tanks is a life and death struggle of cannibalism. The tadpole survives and flourishes by eating its lessers. The fittest survive. Heaney plays down this fact, or, rather, puts it to one side. Schoolteachers use the frogs to introduce a range of facts from sexuality to weather. The naivety of early childhood and the controlled way in which teachers and parents work to painlessly introduce deeper and darker facts about life is well described in the first section of the poem. At the same time, the deliberately naive 'daddy frog' and 'mammy frog' in a sense prepare the reader for the inevitability of a movement away from such innocence. We cannot completely forget that the poem had opened with a succession of unpleasant images: 'festered', 'rotted', 'sweltered', 'the punishing sun'. The second section quickly and comprehensively destroys that innocence, which, after all, was a distortion of the true nature of things. Paradoxically, the flax-dam is still the same place, approached now through fields 'rank / With cowdung'. It is the boy's perception of the grown frogs which has changed.

They have outgrown the creatures which he had been happy to squeeze through his hands as a 'thick warm slobber'. Now the 'great slime kings' assert their dominance of their territory. Of course, there is no actual, physical threat to even a small child from frogs. Again, it is in the boy's imagination that the fear is generated, in a sense, irrationally. Except that the fear and repulsion he feels is not so much a product of the physical threat to himself, it is more that he is now confronted by a realisation that life is not what it seems; that life is about change, flux, maturation and transformation. What he is realising is that the transformation of the frogs is prefiguring the process which we all, inevitably, have to endure. The 'coarse croaking' and 'bass chorus' is an ironical intimation of the trauma of an adolescent boy's voice breaking into manhood.

5 *Summarise my responses to the poem.*

This is a poem which evokes an example of the natural world which our 'civilised' lives deal with most comfortably in a controlled situation. It is specifically concerned with childhood, the innocence of learning and the inevitability of a progression (perhaps a 'fall') into experience. In its theme it is entirely within the tradition of English Romanticism. In a sense, Seamus Heaney has written anew one of Blake's *Songs of Innocence and Experience*; again, this incident would not seem out of place in Wordsworth's long autobiographical poem *The Prelude*.

While *Death of a Naturalist* is essentially traditional, it does foreshorten or condense the theme of innocence moving into experience and in its tone and diction it is clearly contemporary, of our age. In Wordsworth's description, in *The Prelude*, of his guilt at stealing a rowing boat, in his expression of awe in the ascent of Snowdon, or of one of his walks in the Lake District, the poetry is charged with an emotional energy. Heaney's poem employs what might be seen as a more modern detachment. His tone is blunt, 'weighted down by huge sods', then ironical, 'Miss Walls would tell us how / The daddy frog was called a bull frog,' and, finally, frightened and disillusioned, 'if I dipped my hand the spawn would clutch it'. Nevertheless, the poem works very effectively in that it builds up a totally convincing account of a childhood experience; by employing a range of prosodic skills to heighten the evocative power of the memory of the flax-dam and the classroom it also succeeds in dealing with the excitement, confusion and pain of growing up.

II

WATER
by Leslie Norris

On hot summer mornings my aunt set glasses
On a low wall outside the farmhouse,
With some jugs of cold water.
I would sit in the dark hall, or
                    Behind the dairy window,
Waiting for children to come from the town.

They came in small groups, serious, steady,
And I could see them, black in the heat,
Long before they turned in at our gate
To march up the soft, dirt road.
                    They would stand by the wall,
Drinking water with an engrossed thirst. The dog

Did not bother them, knowing them responsible
Travellers. They held in quiet hands their bags
Of jam sandwiches, and bottles of yellow fizz.
Sometimes they waved a gratitude to the house,
                    But they never looked at us.
Their eyes were full of the mountain, lifting

Their measuring faces above our long hedge.
When they had gone I would climb the wall,
Looking for them among the thin sheep runs.
Their heads were a resolute darkness among ferns,
                    They climbed with unsteady certainty.
I wondered what it was they knew the mountain had.

They would pass the last house, Lambert's, where
A violent gander, too old by many a Christmas,
Blared evil warning from his bitten moor,
Then it was open world, too high and clear
                    For clouds even, where over heather
The free hare cleanly ran, and the summer sheep.

I knew this; and I knew all summer long
Those visionary gangs passed through our lanes,
Coming down at evening, their arms full
Of cowslips, moon daisies, whinberries, nuts,
     All fruits of the sliding seasons,
And the enormous experience of the mountain

That I who loved it did not understand.
In the summer, dust filled our winter ruts
With a level softness, and children walked
At evening through golden curtains scuffed
     From the road by their trailing feet.
They would drink tiredly at our wall, talking

Softly, leaning, their sleepy faces warm for home.
We would see them murmur slowly through our stiff
Gate, their shy heads gilded by the last sun.
One by one we would gather up the used jugs,
     The glasses. We would pour away
A little water. It would lie on the thick dust, gleaming.

1   *What sort of writing is shaped in front of me?*

This is a poem of 48 lines, written in 8 verses of 6 lines. Each
line begins with a capital letter. The fifth line of each verse, is,
however, indented, though it does not necessarily indicate the
beginning of a new sentence. Half of the verses run their final
sentence into the beginning of the following verse.

2   *Speak the poem to myself.*

The poem is delivered in the first person and is a memory of
a boy who has either lived with his aunt on her farm, or who
regularly stayed there with her. The story unfolds clearly and
seems almost banal until the last three verses, particularly from
'Those visionary gangs' of verse 6, a phrase to which I shall have
to return, and which suggests that I shall have to re-examine my
initial assumptions about the tone and intention of the poem. I
can perceive no regularity of rhyme, although there are sound
echoes, especially in the fifth verse – 'where', 'moor', 'clear' and
'heather'. Line 4 of the sixth verse,

Of cowslips, moon daisies, whinberries, nuts,

gave me particular pleasure to read aloud. The poem's nostalgic, meditative qualities demand a steady, even slow, pace of reading. Leslie Norris, once again, appears to be a poet who relishes the sound of words and the resonances he is able to set up within lines.

3   *What patterns can I see in the poem?*

I have already pointed out the fact that this poem is organised into eight six-line verses, but also that the fact that half these verses run on into the next verse sets up an interesting tension between the line patterns and the unfolding of the narrative. So, too, the shortened, indented fifth line of each verse does not appear to function according to any syntactical plan; in the second verse it signals a new sentence, but at no other point is its purpose so obvious. In the first verse it is as if the poet were hesitating, working to remember important details. In the third verse the indentations emphasise the peripheral role of the poet and his aunt to the visitors who have come to the mountain. The fifth verse uses its indentation so that we take in the 'high and clear', 'open world' that is above 'clouds even'; we are given time to raise our eyes to the height of the mountain. In the final verse the penultimate line effectively breaks a short sentence – 'The glasses' being separated from 'the used jugs'; the action is distinct, precise, implying the care one would take with such things. The precision also prepares us for the detail of pouring away the remaining drops of water, an image whose effectiveness I shall discuss in a moment.

I have pointed out that there is no formal rhyming pattern in the poem, but Leslie Norris does work towards achieving a pair of near-rhymes or even a couplet in most of his verses. For example, 'water/ or' in the first verse; 'heat/ gate' in the second; in the third, 'bags/ fizz'; in the fourth, 'runs/ ferns'. I have already mentioned the four imperfect rhymes of the next verse, while the sixth verse has 'lanes' and 'mountain' and its fourth line ending 'nuts' finds a perfect rhyme in verse 7 and 'ruts'. 'Sun' and 'home' are the closest sounds in the final verse. What does all this tell us about Norris's craft and intentions in the poem?

Well, he is evidently choosing to rhyme in a variety of ways, both perfectly and imperfectly, and the effect of this is to play upon the reader's visual and aural impression of the poem as an ordered text. *Water* looks and sounds poetic, while not in any way detracting from its contemporaneity and the strength and purpose of its narrative. It has the quality of both poetry and the short story; I mean the modern short story which employs the epiphany, the ending which leaves the reader on the edge of some realisation, just as it leaves the protagonist at the edge of truth or self-knowledge. As we have seen before in the poems we have considered, modern poets, recognising the dangers of too slavish a worship of the formal traditions which characterised Victorian and Edwardian poetry, are often working to hold their poems in a tension between traditional poetic qualities and the appeal of the natural speaking voice with its everyday speech rhythms.

4   *Discuss any ambiguities or paradoxes in the poem.*

The title of this poem seems as straightforward as can be; the poem *is* about water. But it is about water in the same way that baptism or drowning 'is about water'. We will have to clarify the relevance of the title, and, by so doing, we shall surely come to the central purpose of the poem. The sun and water are essential to life and so the act of offering water to the thirsty is one of the basic human kindnesses. In this instance, the poet's aunt would supply 'jugs of cold water' to the walkers and climbers drawn by the warm summer days to the mountain beneath which she lived. At first the walkers are presented as rather typical town children,

> . . . They held in quiet hands their bags
> Of jam sandwiches, and bottles of yellow fizz.

Their sustenance is to be sweet food and manufactured drink; but their eyes 'were full of the mountain' from which they later descend, 'their arms full / Of cowslips, moon daisies, whinberries, nuts', and 'their shy heads gilded by the last sun'. They have been transformed by the experience of the mountain and have become 'visionary gangs' all too grateful for the water provided at the farm wall. The 'engrossed thirst' which they brought with them has been initially satisfied by the farm's water, but more profoundly fed by the experience of climbing the mountain. That deeper thirst has been an emotional, even spiritual one. It is an experience which, paradoxically, the poet as a boy, and perhaps his aunt, may not share even though they live at the very foot of the mountain. It is as if they are too close to appreciate the strangeness of the mountain and its power to affect visitors who, in any case,

> . . . never looked at us.
> Their eyes were full of the mountain, lifting
> Their measuring faces above our long hedge.

As the 'visionary gangs' recede upwards and away he notes their 'unsteady certainty', their heads, 'a resolute darkness among ferns', and both of these images seem strange. 'Unsteady' and yet 'certain' – well, their footing would be unsteady as they climbed, but they nevertheless have an air of resolution in the way they push upwards through the ferns. The darkness of their heads bobbing through the ferns enables the young Norris to focus on the climbers, despite the distance which now lies between them and the farm; though, as far as the significance of their climb is concerned, we might expect them to be gaining light, insight.

The 'violent gander' at Lamberts', 'the last house', blares an 'evil warning' before the climbers break out into an 'open world'. The gander is like some monster in a myth of discovery. He must be braved before the fruits of the mountain may be gatherd. All of this the young Norris sees and, because he loves the mountain, he empathises with the visitors.

It is one of the most common features of autobiographical writing that the narrator feigns the innocence of his earlier years. His task is to convince the reader of that innocence for the duration of the poem or chapter. The reader shares with the writer a knowingness about the wider context of life, but is persuaded to willingly suspend that wider knowledge in order to share the experience of the protagonist. So, in *Water*, Norris creates and maintains a tension between the formative sensual pleasures of the boyhood experience – 'the level softness' of the dust in the ruts of the road, the 'golden curtains scuffed' up by 'their trailing feet' – and the fuller understanding of hindsight as he now realises the pleasures which 'the visionary gangs' seek. That phrase mixes the

Wordsworthian view of nature as the great restorer and the somewhat derogatory 'gangs' with its connotation of an aimless group
of people. Again, there is a tension held between the possibility
of this memory having profound significance, and the sense that
it may be anecdotal, personal, an indulgence by the writer. Of
course, the sort of expectation that we have of any poem is that we
will have revealed to us some insight, a further truth about life.
In a sense, Norris is implicitly relying on that reader expectation
as William Carlos Williams was in 'This is just to say', from
Chapter 1. Unlike the earlier poet, though, Leslie Norris provides
a fuller, more obvious resolution to both his poem and the reader's
needs. Where William's 'Forgive me / they were delicious / so
sweet / and so cold' has a teasing playfulness and relies on tone of
voice, the closing image of *Water* is visual, simple. It, too, owes
much to its shape on the page, the way that 'The glasses' and 'A
little water' are distinguished at the beginning of the last two
lines. The line-break at 'away / A little water' effectively emphasises the precious quality of the water drops which become jew-
elled by 'the last sun' as they are set in 'the thick dust'. It is as if
the boy and his aunt have ministered to the climbers like priests
to pilgrims. The water functions rather like communion wine. The
poem has taken us from the urban banality of 'jam sandwiches, and
bottles of yellow fizz' to a simple act the purity and significance
of which Wordsworth might well have appreciated. The apparent
confusion of references and, therefore, tone has been deliberate
and by the end of the poem should be no longer ambiguous.

5   *Summarise my responses to the poem.*

Water is an autobiographical poem describing a time in the
poet's boyhood which he can recall, or at least recreate, in
precise and evocative detail. The recreation of his days living
on his aunt's farm might well have been retold in a chapter of an
autobiography. However, the memory is particularly enhanced by
its development into a poem because the discipline of the poem's
form concentrates the poet's memory on the core of the experience. We know nothing of the narrator's age, his wider family
situation – is he orphaned and living with his aunt? Is he staying
with her simply over weekends in the summer? Where is this
town and this mountain? When do these events take place? Such
details would be necessary in a prose autobiography or novel, but

are extraneous to the purpose of the poem. By concentrating on the details of the boy's perceptions of the visitors from the town the poet preserves his innocence of the deeper significance of the climbers' 'pilgrimage' to the mountain. We are convinced by the depth of the impression which these days have made upon Norris, but share with him the need to reconsider and evaluate the experience over a distance of time. Perhaps the key line of the poem is the opening of the seventh verse:

> That I who loved it did not understand.

I think that Norris is saying that love and understanding are distinct and that one can exist without the other. He loves 'the enormous experience of the mountain' and, wanting to share that love, he and his aunt provide water to help the town visitors to participate in that 'enormous experience'. The boy, in a sense, renews his own love of the mountain by witnessing in detail the progress that the other children make as they ascend the mountain, and, finally, by his clearing away the water jugs and glasses. The final image of the beads of water reflecting light is a fitting climax to what has become a sort of ritual, a farmhouse wall communion, both in the literal and religious sense. This is a poem which recreates a specific experience, but which, through its evocative detail and disciplined organisation of language and narrative, succeeds in creating for the reader a sense of holiness that is barely tangible, but nonetheless precious.

III

IN THE THEATRE
A True Incident
by Dannie Abse

'Only a local anaesthetic was given because of the blood pressure problem. The patient, thus, was fully awake throughout the operation. But in those days – in 1938, in Cardiff, when I was Lambert Rogers' dresser – they could not locate a brain tumour with precision. Too much normal brain tissue was destroyed as the surgeon crudely searched for it, before he felt

the resistence of it . . . all somewhat hit and miss. One operation I shall
never forget . . . . '

(Dr Wilfred Abse)

Sister saying – 'Soon you'll be back in the ward,'
sister thinking – 'Only two more on the list,'
the patient saying – 'Thank you, I feel fine';
small voices, small lies, nothing untoward,
though, soon, he would blink again and again   5
because of the fingers of Lambert Rogers,
rash as a blind man's, inside his soft brain.

If items of horror can make a man laugh
then laugh at this: one hour later, the growth
still undiscovered, ticking its own wild time;   10
more brain mashed because of the probe's braille path;
Lambert Rogers desperate, fingering still;
his dresser thinking, 'Christ! Two more on the list,
a cisternal puncture and a neural cyst.'

Then, suddenly, the cracked record in the brain,   15
a ventriloquist voice that cried, 'You sod,
leave my soul alone, leave my soul alone,' –
the patient's dummy lips moving to that refrain,
the patient's eyes too wide. And shocked,
Lambert Rogers drawing out the probe   20
with nurses, students, sister, petrified.

'Leave my soul alone, leave my soul alone,'
that voice so arctic and that cry so odd
had nowhere else to go – till the antique
gramophone wound down and the words began   25
to blur and slow, ' . . . leave . . . my . . . soul . . .
                                          alone . . . '
to cease at last when something other died.
And silence matched the silence under snow.

1   *What sort of writing is shaped in front of me?*

This is a poem of 28 lines comprising 4 verses of 7 lines. There
is a subtitle and a prose passage attributed to 'Dr Wilfred Abse'.

The 'theatre' is obviously an operating theatre in a hospital. I feel that the prose passage will probably indicate a specific historical context, and help to persuade the reader of the 'documentary' validity of the events presented by the poem. Both the attribution to Dr Abse and the passage itself are italicised, in common with the subtitle. Clearly, something about this poem requires substantiation. Some readers may be irritated by the prose detail, and some intrigued by the implications of the introduction. In a way, the prose passage acts as a phantom verse in this poem; the unfinished final sentence fades out rather as a voice-over in a television film might precede the dramatisation of an incident.

2   *Speak the poem to myself.*

The most striking aspect of this poem as a performance piece is the number of voices one has to render. First, there's the evidence of Dr Wilfred Abse, then the nursing sister with her public and internal voice, the patient, Lambert Rogers' dresser (I take this to be a wound dresser assisting at the operation), and, finally, the chilling ghost-voice of the patient's 'soul'. I can immediately relate this to the title of the poem for, in a way, the operating theatre becomes a theatre of voices, a radio theatre at least, with the narrator (the poet, I suppose) presenting the drama of this ghastly operation. The poet has given us the information necessary to our performing the various voice-parts, but it is a challenging task. Certainly, a public reading / performance of this poem would tax most readers. The 'stage-directions' in the final verse for the words 'to blur and slow' might cause particular concern. This is a frightening prospect as one associates with the patient, and I, for one, felt self-conscious in attempting that winding-down sound of the brain's coherence.

   The use of semi-colons and dashes throughout the poem may present some readers with problems of how to read the lines. However, the power of the dramatic elements of the poem should soon establish the pace and direction of the narrative. There are rhymes evident from even a first reading, though the regularity of these may be problematic. Certainly, the final verse has an insistent 'o' sound – 'alone . . . so . . . no- . . . go . . . slow . . . soul . . . alone . . . snow' which adds to the drama of the patient's suffering.

3   *What patterns can I see in the poem?*

The four verses of the poem effectively present the story in four stages, from the reassurance of the sister as the patient is wheeled to the operating theatre; then the further details of 'the fingers of Lambert Rogers, / rash as a blind man's, inside his soft brain' in the second verse which suspends the tension somewhat by the dresser's concern about the cases remaining for that day; the third verse deals in detail with the moment of obvious damage and the final verse outlines the horrible completion of the patient's tragedy. Thus, the poem has the narrative force of a play or fiction, with the effective suspension of progress and the consequent raising of tension for the reader.

It is difficult to outline a strictly regular rhyme-scheme in the poem, though each verse has at least two pairs of perfect or imperfect rhyming line-endings. So, in the first verse 'ward / untoward' and 'again / brain' suggest possibilities of a strict rhyme pattern, but that pattern is resolutely prevented by 'Rogers' and 'list', and also by the consonant rhyme of 'fine' with 'again' and 'brain'. However, there are further complications, for the parallelism of the first three lines –

> Sister saying . . .
> sister thinking . . .
> the patient saying . . .

and the fourth line's repetition, 'small voices, small lies,' are at least as important in establishing the terms of the poem: I think that these characteristics of syntax, especially the effect of the caesuras in the first four lines, create a sense of the patient's isolation and his distance from the others' perceptions of the situation.

In the second verse the concluding couplet effectively undercuts the unease that has been created by the horror of the operation and the imperfect rhymes – 'laugh . . . growth . . . path'. The blasphemous 'Christ!' is occasioned only by the inconvenience of the delay in progressing through the operating list, though it is the patient whose brain is 'mashed because of the probe's braille path' who is most in need of Christ's intervention. The consonantal rhyming of 'Christ' with 'list' and 'cyst' is darkly ironical. The sister had reassured herself with the thought 'Only two more on the list'; now, the dresser recalls that fact almost in despair.

In verse 3 the practice of withholding perfect line-ending rhymes is continued with 'probe' and 'shocked' only faintly linking with the shock of 'sod' in the second line. However, the internal rhyme of 'wide' and 'petrified' is striking as the patient's staring eyes and his outburst confront the operating team with the clumsiness of their well-meaning efforts.

In the final verse 'alone', in line 22, is repeated as a line-ending and links with 'began', in line 25, but of far more importance is the insistent repetition of the 'o' sounds that was immediately *heard* in our reading of the poem. This sound builds up most dramatically to the last word of the poem and the aptness of that final image

> And silence matched the silence under snow.

The patient is buried, his personality obliterated. He has become the *tabula rasa*, a blankness from which his illness and the operation has removed all significance. The final stages of his disappearance as a person are horribly indicated by the assonance of the poem's conclusion, especially the lines

> . . . the antique
> gramophone wound down and the words began
> to blur and slow, ' . . . leave . . . my . . . soul . . . alone . . . '

He drifts out of existence as our breath exhales in the pronunciation of those vowels, until, with the repetition of silence and the completion of the 'slow / snow' rhyme, he finally disappears.

4   *Discuss any ambiguities or paradoxes in the poem.*

I have already noted the double intention of the title; the poem is, in fact, also functioning as a play for voices. Each of the four verses includes direct speech and these voices, in addition to that of the narrator, lend the poem a peculiar quality of drama. They draw the reader into the situation as perceived by the various protagonists. There is also the question of the way in which the prose extract functions. Although some readers may welcome the documentary authority which such an introduction lends the poem which follows, there is an equally strong reaction which would see the prose as in some way detracting from the 'purity' of the poem. I suppose that the details of the surgeon's failure and the crudity of the brain operation are so horrifying that it is some consolation to have these events accurately located some 30 years ago when such radical surgery was in its infancy. The implication is, surely, that such a thing could not happen to us. It would be profoundly disturbing to have our faith in the medical profession shaken in this way; after all, many successful brain operations do now take place as a matter of course in our hospitals. There is one other effect created by the prose passage: the poet is presenting the fact that he is himself reacting to a story told to him. He is both narrator and audience. Or, perhaps, he becomes narrator after having been the audience for the original recounting of the experience. This function will, of course, be again altered if we encounter the poem as being attributed to Dannie Abse. In that case, 'Dr Wilfred Abse' becomes related as father, uncle, or brother to the poet. We may then begin to imagine this story as one which the poet has himself been impressed and frightened by as he listened to an older member of his family.

The apparent paradox of the sister's words of reassurance and the actual nature of the operation which the patient is shortly to undergo is, we must surely recognise, a common experience in hospitals. Both patient and staff share a code of references which rely on euphemism, understatement and platitude; that is the way both sides usually prefer it. Within the terms of this poem the platitudes succeed in delaying and therefore increasing the shock effect of the operation itself –

> . . . the fingers of Lambert Rogers,
> rash as a blind man's, inside his soft brain.

The paradox is that it is the surgeon who is 'blind' and the helpless patient who can perceive all too clearly what is happening to him. Rogers' probe in fact ploughs a 'braille path' through the 'mashed' brain. The dark irony of this is underlined by the opening lines of the second verse where Abse seems to accuse us all of regarding horror too flippantly; our nervous laughter covers up the threat to our security; it often helps us to avoid the potential embarrassment of having to empathise with victims. He then tests our resilience in the face of his particular story of horror as the tumour, 'ticking its own wild time', is beyond the scope of the theatre staff's skill and redefines their sense of time.

In the third verse, the man on the operating table has become transformed into a ventriloquist's dummy who no longer speaks, but whose lips move to the clumsy prompting of Lambert Rogers, the 'blind man' who opens the eyes of his patient 'too wide'. Paradoxically, it is the medical team who are immobilised, 'petrified', and the patient who is animated. It is almost as if he speaks in tongues, like a visionary who has glimpsed some vast spiritual truth and who transmits that truth to a congregation. Except that the soul of this man cries out 'You sod,' and continues to shout 'leave my soul alone' until, like an 'antique / gramophone wound down', he loses even that power to assert his entity. In the heat of the theatre, after this long operation, that voice is as cold as the arctic and the chill that emanates from the patient chills all who witness it, including the readers of the poem. That happens 'when something other died'. What else could that be but the soul? The soul, the core of our being as individuals, finds expression most subtly through language, and so this poem addresses the question of language and the way in which it is precariously carried in our bodies, susceptible to the body's frailty and ultimate mortality. By making his reader *sound out* the final fading words of this doomed man Dannie Abse implicates us in that vulnerability. The pause after that final 'snow' seems absolute. The line could be, perhaps grammatically *should* be, part of the previous sentence. By disjointing it, Abse stresses the depth of the isolation we all face beyond language.

5   *Summarise my responses to the poem.*

This poem is a disturbing piece of writing only partly mitigated by its historical setting. Abse retells, in painful detail, the chilling consequences of an operation that went wrong. I would suppose that most of us are susceptible to such frightening revelations and Abse works to undermine our complacency about life and our often naïve reliance on medicine. He reminds us of our mortality and, further, he reminds us that whatever higher ideals we may have, whatever beliefs in the survival of the soul we may wrest from our religious observances, we must recognise that our bodies are all we know for certain in this life. Lambert Rogers' 'probe's braille' destroys a man, his personality and, for all we know, his soul itself. Is this then a poem of extreme pessimism, even nihilism? I think not. Finally, what Abse achieves is a deepening of our regard for life. At the end of this poem we are left with the knowledge that everyone is affected by death and suffering: from Lambert Rogers, the surgeon who presides over the world of the hospital, to the patient, prone and helpless, an Everyman who represents us all. The poem concludes before the story has finished. What happens to the theatre staff and the patient when the 'antique gramophone' is completely wound down? Of course, it is a necessary part of the poem's effect that we should be left on the edge of that dilemma. For the patient, 'silence matched the silence under snow'. There is no more. It is the poet's intention to lead us up to the edge of an abyss, silent, full of snow; there we stand, made to face the possibility of a vast nothingness. The security of our society, its professional expertise, its hospitals and research are put into perspective by that silence. *In the theatre* confronts readers, finally, with themselves.

6

The 1980s

THE three poets, Seamus Heaney, Leslie Norris and Dannie
Abse, considered in the previous chapter are still active writers
adding to their already considerable body of work as the eighth
decade of this century comes to a close. The Liverpool poets
whom I mentioned in Chapter 4 also continue to publish, but
their influence may now be seen to have been more central to the
exposure and projection of poetry readings than in the creation of
a lasting 'pop' poetry. But there have been other developments in
poetry which are of interest.

In the late 1970s a new poetry 'movement' was recognised
by the media and various critics. This was 'Martian Poetry'
and it focused on Craig Raine and a number of other young
poets. Raine's first collection was called *A Martian Sends a Postcard Home*. Critics applauded the cleverness of the imagery in
this collection and in the poetry of Christopher Reid, Michael
Hoffman, Mathew Sweeney and others. Comparisons were made
with the seventeenth-century 'Metaphysical Poets' such as John
Donne whose poetry was characterised by its witty, often oblique
and convoluted similes. An extended simile was a 'metaphysical
conceit' which displayed the poet's cleverness and originality.
Certainly, in the best poems by Raine and his contemporary
'Martians' there is a challenging sense of confronting an enig-
ma, of decoding signs partially recognised and understood. That
element of the puzzle has always been involved in poetry; the
Anglo-Saxons had a genre of poem-riddles and the Japanese
Haiku often has that quality. In a poem such as *The Man Who
Invented Pain*, from Craig Raine's 1984 collection *Rich*, I think
that the cleverness is harnessed to a real concern for the
First World War private executed for mistakenly liberating the
carrier pigeons vital to communications from the trenches. Each
detail of the man's last day is delivered with a witty comparison
that stresses the uniqueness of each experience, no matter how

banal, and thus intensifies the sense of stupidity and loss as the execution is carried out.

In general, though, I feel that the media over-reacted to the phenomenon of the 'Martians' in the late 1970s and early 1980s in much the same way that had occurred when the 'Movement' was created in the 1950s. There undoubtedly were fine poems produced by Raine, Reid and Hofmann at this time, but the sort of image making for which they were praised had been achieved, notably by the Scottish poet Norman MacCaig, throughout the post-war period. At its most shallow it was no more than a college-clever extension of the punning popularised by the Liverpool Poets. There is a greater achievement to be found, I think, in the narrative, often historically researched poetry of Andrew Motion in Britain and Norman Dubie in the USA.

The three poets I have chosen to consider in this chapter are outstanding writers whose best work may still be to come. They also represent writing backgrounds to which we may well look for the best poetry remaining in this century. Fred D'Aguiar is a young black poet, born in London, presently based in Brixton, but brought up in Guyana. Gillian Clarke is one of the most notable of a number of outstanding women poets who have found the post-feminist publishing situation a more welcoming one. There are probably more collections of poems by women published in Britain and the USA in any one month now than you could have catalogued in the whole of the nineteenth century. Paul Muldoon is notable among a group of young men and women poets who have followed Seamus Heaney, Michael Longley and Derek Mahon as remarkable voices speaking from troubled Ireland.

I

MAMA DOT WARNS AGAINST AN EASTER RISING
by Fred D'Aguiar

Doan raise no kite is good friday
but is out he went out an fly it
us thinkin maybe dere wont be a breeze
strong enouf an widout any a we to hole it
fo him he'd neva manage to get it high-up   5

to de tree top ware de wind kissin
de ripess sweetess fruit we cawn reach
but he let out some string bit by bit
tuggin de face into de breeze
coaxin it up all de time takin a few steps back   10
an it did rise up bit by bit till de lang tail
din't touch de groun an we grip de palin
we head squeeze between to watch him
an trace its rise rise rise up up up in de sky
we all want to fly in like bird but can only kite   15
fly an he step back juss as we beginnin
to smile fo him envy him his easter risin
when bap he let out a scream leggo string
an de kite drop outta de sky like a bird
a sail down to de nex field an we runnin to him   20
forgetting de kite we uncle dem mek days ago
fram wood shave light as bird bone
paper tin like fedder an de tongue o kite
fo singin in de sky like a bird an de tail
fo balance string in de mout like it pullin   25
de longess worm an he a hole him foot
an a bawl we could a see seven inch a greenhart
gone in at de heel runnin up him leg
like a vein he groanin all de way to de haspital
on de cross-bar a bike ridden by a uncle   30
she not saying a word but we hearin her
fo de ress a dat day an evry year since
doan raise no kite is good friday
an de sky was a birdless kiteless wait fo her word

1   *What kind of writing is shaped in front of me?*

The left-hand justification and lack of right-hand justification
indicates that this is a poem. It has 34 lines, 2 of which are
italicised. These are the command of Mama Dot; the first time
'Doan' had a capital letter which opens the poem. There is
no other capital letter, nor is there any punctuation. This is
obviously not written in conventional English, apart from its
title. The strangeness of the spelling and the absence of clear
sentences is disturbing, and seem to indicate that reading this

poem aloud (never mind readily understanding it) may prove far from straightforward.

2 Speak the poem to myself.

This does, indeed, prove difficult. Certainly, there is no possibility of voicing this poem without projecting oneself into the character of a Caribbean child. (I hardly think that most readers would fail to recognise the source of this poem's language.) Of course, the West Indian accent is familiar to those of us who live in Britain. The influence of that distinctive use of language, becoming the predominant dialect of some areas even, is now no longer a foreign one as the immigrants of the 1950s become integrated into the complexity that is multi-racial Britain of the 1980s. In popular music and entertainment as well as sport the West Indian character is readily recognised. What happens when we try to sound out the poem is that we unconsciously decode the language and 'read' it as standard English. Thus, '*Doan raise no kite is good friday*' becomes, 'Don't fly any of your kites – today is Good Friday'. This process of translation is instant and will not necessarily slow down or perceptibly weaken the flow of the lines and the narrative. Still, one might want to question the value of such an exercise. What, we might ask, would the poem lose if it were written in the English which is standard for most of us? Well, that translation of the first line which I have just attempted does seem somehow less effective, doesn't it? It is unlikely that many mothers or grandmothers in this country would utter such words in 'received' English anyway. The way we speak to each other is further from the formal use of language in its written form than we might realise. So much is involved in communication that goes beyond language: the raising of an eyebrow, the clenching of a fist, the widening of an eye, the stance of our bodies – all these things are signals to others and interact with language. One of the problems that a poet faces is to represent the character and attitude of a narrator and other protagonists without the benefit of a stage or screen and actors, and without the lengthy asides which a novelist may use. While an actor may, speaking in an accent, immediately establish the locality of the play, both novelists and poets have to find other means of doing that. Moving away from standard English is the obvious step.

There is, though, a problem in doing that; the writer may risk confusing and antagonising the reader. I am always infuriated when the character Joseph appears in Emily Brontë's *Wuthering Heights*. She chooses to transcribe his thick Yorkshire accent with a determination for accuracy which may be justified in geographic terms, but which, effectively, brings the narrative to a dead slow. What are we to make of the following?

'Eech! eech! Weel done, Miss Cathy! weel done, Miss Cathy! Hahsiver, t'maister sall just tum'le o'er them brocken pots; un' then we's hear summut; we's hear hah it's tu be. Gooid-for-nowt madling! yah deserve pining froo this to Churstmas, flinging t'precious gifts uh God under fooit i' yer flkaysome rages! Bud Aw'm mista'en if yah shew yer sperrit lang. Will Hathecliff bide such bonny ways, think ye? Aw nobbut wish he muh cotch ye i' that plisky. Aw nobbut wish he may.
(*Wuthering Heights*, Chapter 13, Penguin, 1967, p.180.)

This passage takes several readings in order to understand; and several more before we would want to read it aloud before a class of students.

Let me give you just one more example of this sort of problem. Shakespeare's portrayal of Fluellen in *Henry V* may be an attempt at a regional British accent which those who live in Wales may find less than amusing, look you.

To the mines! Tell you the Duke it is not so good to come to the mines; for, look you, the mines is not according to the disciplines of war; the concavities of it is not sufficient. For, look you, th' athversary — you may discuss unto the Duke, look you — is digt himself four yard under the countermines; by Cheshu, i think 'a will plow up all, if there is not better directions.

(III, ii.)

There is, then, a long tradition of utilising accent in writing, from the regional variants of Middle English down to D. H. Lawrence and Alan Sillitoe, though national and regional groups may feel that they are satirised in some way by the portrayal of their accents in written English. The violent outcry which greeted the stories of Caradoc Evans in 1913 is a prime example: when his play *Taffy* was produced in London the London Welsh society bought up most of the tickets and sang hymns to completely drown the performance. Nevertheless, the effect of this strategy on the reader is invariably marked, and in each of the examples above it would have been absurd to represent the speech of Joseph or Fluellen in the received or BBC English of its age.

Fred D'Aguiar challenges us to see and hear in the accent of the West Indian child as a natural and therefore valid form of expression. The absence of punctuation and the elision of many of the words – 'enouf', 'ripess', 'nex' – does not, I think, put too much strain on the reader, and does succeed in conveying a special kind of naivety and excitement. The poem is about excitement, a 'rising' against which Mama Dot delivers a sombre warning. I should also note at this early stage that the vocabulary is appropriately limited in this poem; and that some words are repeated several times through the poem – 'bird', 'sky', 'fly' – as if the elements of the story were what the child needs to return to constantly.

3   What patterns can I see in the poem?

The most obvious device is the return to Mama Dot's opening warning at the end of the poem. There appears to be no rhyme-scheme, though there are fortuitous rhymes and imperfect rhymes at certain points – 'palin / him', 'beginnin / risin / string', 'kite / foot'. Also, one hears internal rhymes – 'sky . . . fly', 'bawl . . . heel', 'runnin . . . vein . . . groanin'. The lyric strengths of this poem lie, rather, in the repetition of those basic words and in the musicality of the accent implied in the text. It is as if the repetition of the act through the words is re-enacted and, at the same time, celebrated and re-energised. The conjunction 'and' is repeated many times, as it would be in the excited retelling of a story by a child.

4   Discuss any ambiguities or paradoxes in the poem.

The title of the poem is certainly ambiguous in that 'Easter rising' reminds me of the poem by W. B. Yeats, *Easter Rising, 1916.* That famous poem celebrates the Irish attempt to take the city of Dublin and force the British government to recognise home rule for Ireland. Yeats was a romantic and a nationalist (he eventually became a senator in the new Republic of Eire).

But Fred D'Aguiar's poem turns out not to be about politics at all; at least I fail to see how the kite flying could be political, unless there is some deeply rooted allegory in the story. Perhaps Mama Dot represents the mother country and the children are a new generation who disobey her commands and determine to escape her dominance by their act of defiance? Well, that does seem far-fetched, doesn't it? But we should recognise the fact that there is always the possibility of chasing such red herrings when a reader is sent in the wrong direction by a misreading of title or text, or a distorting weight of emphasis that their own prejudice insists. In this instance, a calm, sensible reading of the poem should lead the reader to the conclusion that Fred D'Aguiar has written an autobiographical poem that is also a character poem, because Mama Dot is the dominant figure of the poem, even though she is heard only twice, reiterating the one command. The title plays with the echo of the Yeats poem, but also uses the same connotation which drew Yeats to that title in the first place: it is Christ who rose at Easter. Easter is the Christian festival of celebration for that resurrection of Christ. Yeats was determined to associate the martyrdom of his nationalist rebels with the greatest sacrifice that our culture acknowledges. Fred D'Aguiar, on the other hand, is more concerned with creating an image of children's need to be adventurous, to break rules, to go against what they are told is 'sensible'. As with the poems which we have read by Seamus Heaney and Leslie Norris, the poetry is making a statement about something very central to our experience by re-creating an incident from his memory of childhood.

The largest problem facing the reader of the poem, as we have seen, is in dealing with the particular form of English Fred D'Aguiar uses. There are occasions when the combination of the dialect and the lack of punctuation demand a second or third reading simply to establish the basic meaning of the line or sentence. For example, the lines from 'to smile fo him envy him . . . ' to 'we uncle dem mek days ago' are impossible to read coherently until one has grasped the effect of that 'bap' (l.18) which is like a cartoon punch or crash. 'De kite we uncle dem mek days ago' (l.21) could mean both 'the kite our uncle made for them days ago', or, 'the kite our uncles made for us days ago'. It would be a harsh marker who penalised any examinee for the confusion which raises from that syntax. That detail is, however, not crucial to the story, nor to the effectiveness of the poem in its treatment of childhood. We should ourselves be unduly harsh in criticising Fred D'Aguiar for ambiguity at that point. More important is the overall effect of the language he uses in creating a totally convincing impression of childhood innocence and excitement.

There are several obvious instances where the poetry is enhanced by the ambiguous nature of the syntax and the diction. For example, when the young kite-flier trips and injures himself in his excitement in lines 26-28:

> . . . he a hole him foot
> an a bawl we could see seven inch a greenhart
> gone in at de heel runnin up him leg

The 'hole him foot' carries a double meaning of the boy *holding* his foot, and also *holing* his foot as the sharp plant pierces him. Here, too, the incident is held in suspension from line 18 to that line 26 by the narrator's desire to describe the kite and the complexity of its construction. The drama of the boy's accident is unconsciously weighed against the awe at the beauty of the kite itself; the story is therefore interrupted in much the way that a playwright like Harold Pinter might create convolutions in the story-telling of one of his characters. That sort of digression is common in our experience of tales in a number of situations, from bus journey to college refectory.

The last line, too, effectively rests on that peculiarity of language. It is a quite original use of the word 'wait': is it a verb or a noun? We have seen in Chapter 3 how Dylan Thomas used that shift of verb and noun; here Fred D'Aguiar implies that the sky was birdless and kiteless, but also that it embodied the expectation and frustration of the children. It is as if the sky were a blank canvas waiting for the kite to brush colour and movement into it.

5   Summarise my responses to the poem.

Mama Dot Warns Against an Easter Rising is a highly unusual and original poem by virtue of its form. The English language of the Caribbean children lends a specially poetic quality to the writing; this is because accent and dialect are strong foregrounding elements in any piece of writing – they focus our attention on the language itself and not simply on the narrative. The reader is thus forced to re-create the voice of the narrator and to inhabit the experience quite directly. That experience is vivid, dramatic and significant. The subtropical landscape is hinted at – 'de ripess sweetess fruit we cawn reach' (l.7) – but not described in detail. It is, rather, the vivid detail of the kite's construction which focuses the boy's excitement; after all, he would take his landscape for granted, wouldn't he? As his gaze fixes on the rising kite, so does ours. We share in the sense of innocent excitement. Then, just as Seamus Heaney's pleasure in the tadpoles in *Death of a Naturalist* is broken down by his experiencing the grown, gross frogs, so Fred D'Aguiar's friend is brought down to earth by the 'seven inch a greenhart' which pierces his heel. Like Achilles in the Greek myth, the boy's weakness is revealed, his moment of magical escape is foreshortened. Like an ancient myth, too, is the foretelling of danger by the wise woman. Mama Dot is the oracle pronouncing 'Doan raise no kite is good friday' as first a warning and then a precept which is renewed each year and which becomes established as a piece of received wisdom. The poem works convincingly as autobiography, but also as an example of the tension between a child's need to grow beyond its parents and their wisdom and the fact that acknowledging that wisdom is an essential part of locating oneself in a family and of claiming a cultural identity. The poem ends with an image which realises that tension; the children and the sky itself 'wait fo her word'.

II

THE HARE
(i.m. Frances Horovitz 1938-1983)
by Gillian Clarke

That March night I remember how we heard
a baby crying in a neighbouring room
but found him sleeping quietly in his cot.

The others went to bed and we sat late
talking of children and the men we loved. 5
You thought you'd like another child. 'Too late'

you said. And we fell silent, thought a while
of yours with his copper hair and mine,
a grown daughter and sons.

Then, that joke we shared, our phases of the moon.   10
'Sisterly lunacy' I said. You liked
the phrase. It became ours. Different

as earth and air, yet in one trace that week
we towed the calends like boats reining
the oceans of the world at full moon.   15

Suddenly from the fields we heard again
a baby cry, and standing at the door
listened for minutes, ears and eyes soon used

to the night. It was cold. In the east
the river made a breath of shining sound.   20
The cattle in the field were shadow black.

A cow coughed. Some slept, and some pulled grass.
I could smell blossom from the blackthorn
and see their thorny crowns against the sky.

And then again, a sharp cry from the hill.   25
'A hare', we said together, not speaking
of fox or trap that held it in a lock

of terrible darkness. Both admitted
next day to lying guilty hours awake
at the crying of the hare. You told me   30

of sleeping at last in the jaws of a bad dream.
"I saw all the suffering of the world
in a single moment. Then I heard

a voice say 'But this is nothing, nothing
to the mental pain'." I couldn't speak of it.   35
I thought about your dream when you lay ill.

In the last heavy nights before full moon,
when its face seems sorrowful and broken,
I look through binoculars. Its seas flower

like clouds over water, it wears its craters   40
like silver rings. Even in dying you
menstruated as a woman in health

considering to have a child or no.
When they hand me insults or little hurts
and I'm on fire with my arguments   45

at your great distance you can calm me still.
Your dream, my sleeplessness, the cattle
asleep under a full moon,

and out there
the dumb and stiffening body of the hare.   50

1   What sort of writing is shaped in front of me?

This is a poem of 50 lines, conventionally punctuated, without
capital letters at the beginning of each line, and comprising 16
verses of 3 lines *(tercets)* and a concluding couplet. The verses
may be end-stopped, or may run on into the following verse.
I am drawn immediately to the fact that there is a subtitle. I
know that 'i.m.' stands for 'in memory of', so must assume that
this poem is an elegy.

2   Speak the poem to myself.

This is a first-person poem spoken by a woman to another
woman. I did not encounter any problems with the syntax or
the diction, except for the image in the fifth verse,

> we towed the calends like boats reining
> the oceans of the world at the full moon.

I have looked up 'calends' in the dictionary and find that these
are the 'First of month in Roman calendar'. I am not clear as to
how that helps me in understanding the image; clearly, I shall
have to return to that problem.
    I was not aware of a rhyme scheme in the poem, though
there was a musicality, a 'poetry' in the sound of language,
and the final two lines *do* rhyme fully. I recognise this as a
not uncommon device in contemporary poetry.

As a man I found this poem a challenge. It is not easy for a man convincingly to perform lines which speak of the direct experience of giving birth and of menstruating. Perhaps I ought to consider for a moment the centuries of poetry by men outlining the exploits and experiences of men with which generations of women have had to deal.

3   What patterns can I see in the poem?

Even if there is no set rhyme pattern, I can still note the poet's desire to elevate language in her poem. In the first seven lines, for example, I can hear the insistence of an 'ight' sound in the words 'night . . . quietly . . . late . . . thought . . . late . . . silent'. In the same lines the same foregrounding of language can be noted with regard to 'room . . . him' and 'children . . . men . . . ' which extends on to 'mine . . . grown . . . sons . . . moon . . . lunacy'. This admixture of consonant rhyme, assonance, imperfect rhymes and internal rhyme is difficult to define or qualify, but it is, nevertheless, the source of that 'poetic' heightening we sense in such writing. Though there are imperfect rhymes at line-endings – 'mine . . . moon', 'moon . . . again', 'flower / craters', and 'still / cattle', the very fact that lines hold back from full rhyming underlines the power of the final rhyming couplet and enforces the conviction of the poet's final point.

There is an underlying narrative pattern in the sense that the poem begins with an image of a baby crying and the notion of conception is followed through the poem, right up to the final scenes of the death of Frances Horovitz and the hare. The poet clearly intends her poem to follow the cyclical shape of life, for there are constant references to the pull of the moon and the cycle of menstruation necessary for procreation. The central tragedy of the poem is tied to these images of birth and blood, night and death.

4   Discuss any ambiguities or paradoxes in the poem.

The poem opens with the presentation of an ambiguous experience – the phantom cry of a baby – which is held as a mystery until the ninth verse when both women in the same instant recognise the cry as that of a hare. The act of recognition is itself another instance of the empathy which Gillian Clarke wants to establish between herself and Frances Horovitz. But that very special relationship is itself the source of some ambiguity and paradox. Such a relationship, a close bonding between human beings is a form of the highest, most intense of human experiences; it qualifies us as human beings: yet such a relationship necessitates the exclusion of others. Perhaps that is the best way of understanding that particularly obtuse image of the 'calends'. When Gillian Clarke talks of her 'sisterly lunacy' with Frances Horovitz she means not only the girlish joke, but that the coincidence of their menstrual cycles, 'one trace', pulls together the months in unison. Through their bodies the moon's pull on the oceans is realised and unified. Exerting such an elemental force, the two women complement each other and complete the whole 'world at full moon'.

In verse two 'The others went to bed . . . ' leaving the two women to talk intimately. In fact, the 'others' who, I suppose, are children, lovers, husbands, do not appear again in the poem. The consideration of the hare and the subsequent coping with Frances's death becomes a shared experience, in the mind of the poet at least, between the two women alone. Now this is a not uncommon stance for a poet to take in a poem. It is rather like the novelist's point of view technique, or the film director's concentration on the emotions and experiences of a single character or small group of characters in the midst of some great catastrophe. There is a sense in which this imbuing of a character with representative force is at the core of nearly all drama and fiction. As I have already noted, the tradition of Romanticism in English literature has often put the poets themselves at the centre of the poem. So, too, at the core of the poem is the need to move instantly and dramatically from the time of the hare's cry to the death of Frances Horovitz. This occurs in the twelfth verse,

I thought about your dream when you lay ill.

The manipulation of time is further complicated in the poem by the switch back to the present and Gillian Clarke's continuing practice of moon gazing. In the thirteenth verse, rather confusingly at first, she moves immediately from the death-bed to the attraction of the 'full moon, / when its face seems sorrowful and broken', the beauty of which she observes through binoculars. I suppose that a reader might take those lines as still located at the time of the friend's death, but transposed into the present tense for the sake of heightening the effect. I favour my original response simply because the poem goes on to draw a continuing and lasting consequence from the experience of the friendship and the death. Gillian Clarke, in the fifteenth and sixteenth verses, stands firm by her commitment to the friendship and the significance of the shared experiences with Frances Horovitz. She says:

> When they hand me insults or little hurts
> and I'm on fire with my arguments
>
> at your great distance you can calm me still.
>
> (lines 44–46.)

The whole relationship lives on in the poet and is re-enacted in her behaviour.

The fact that the last image of the poem is not, in fact, a sentence might cause some confusion. However, the sense of the poem by this stage means that the full-stop after 'still' *has* to be read as a colon. Thus, the calmness which Frances Horovitz can bring to Gillian Clarke is in the way in which her memory comprises the whole of the experience:

> Your dream, my sleeplessness, the cattle
> asleep under a full moon,
>
> and out there
> the dumb and stiffening body of the hare.

That final image catalogues the elements of the experience and becomes emblematic of their relationship. There is, para-doxically, a rightness about the dead hare. It takes its place almost placidly in the landscape of the cattle's grazing under the full moon. (Perhaps this is the justification too for the rather strained image of the crucifixion created by the blackthorn's 'thorny crowns against the sky'. We have been prepared for a sacrifice.) Still, the natural flow of that closing image embodies the resolution that is the poem's purpose; it is what the poet wants to celebrate out of the sorrow of bereavement. This poem, contemporary in its tone and directness, is traditional in its movement towards the reconciliation of complex images and feelings.

5 *Summarise my responses to the poem.*

This a poem by a woman, but not necessarily a feminist poem. Gillian Clarke rests heavily on the English Romantic tradition in the sense that *The Hare* reminds us of lyrics by Wordsworth and Coleridge; poems that deal with universal themes through the recreation of intense personal experience, often shared with family and close friends, and often taking place in a natural landscape of intense beauty, 'In the east / the river made a breath of shining sound.' This poem, however, transfers the sensibility from a male persona to a female. The common fact of menstruation, that positive fact which distinguishes the female from the male of the species, has been characterised as 'the wise wound' by another contemporary poet, and this emphasis on the positive aspects of menstruation is central to the new ideology of Woman in a post-feminist society. The poem relates menstruation to the movement of the moon, and so to the cyclical moving of life itself. It is a blood-bond between the two women, distinguishing them and their relationship from those around them, even their closest family. The implication is that women have a special relationship with the world: in tune with its central movements, they have powers of perception that are special and a commonality on which each may draw

> When they hand me insults or little hurts
> and I'm on fire with my arguments

The response of the two women to the cry of the trapped hare, both 'out there' and 'in the jaws of a bad dream' is one of empathy, of common blood with other creatures. The moon is a constant source of meaning for them, if only they would look for 'Its seas flower / like clouds over water, it wears its craters / like silver rings'. That image sounds a distant echo for us from the rings of 'Aunt Jennifer's fingers' in Adrienne Rich's poem (Chapter 1). It mixes fertility and entrapment; in a sense, *The Hare* is dealing precisely with those themes.

III

CUBA
by Paul Muldoon

My eldest sister arrived home that morning
In her white muslin evening dress.
'Who the hell do you think you are,
Running out to dances in next to nothing?
As though we hadn't enough bother   5
With the world at war, if not at an end.'
My father was pounding the breakfast-table.

'Those Yankees were touch and go as it was –
If you'd heard Patton at Armagh –
But this Kennedy's nearly an Irishman   10
So he's not much better than ourselves.
And him with only to say the word.
If you've got anything on your mind
Maybe you should make your peace with God.'

I could hear May from beyond the curtain.   15
'Bless me, Father, for I have sinned.
I told a lie once, I was disobedient once.
And, Father, a boy touched me once.'
'Tell me, child. Was this touch immodest?
Did he touch your breast, for example?'   20
'He brushed against me, Father. Very gently.'

1   *What sort of writing is shaped in front of me?*

This is a short poem of twenty-one lines comprising three
seven-line verses. The capitalisation convention is followed.
There is a substantial amount of direct speech.

2   *Speak the poem to myself.*

The poem is in the first-person and I take the narrator to be
a man remembering an incident from his childhood. He is Irish
and the setting is Ireland – the reference to Armagh indicates that
this is the north of Ireland. I need to *hear* that region's accent in
order to correctly receive the particular tone and emphasis of the

speech. The fact that I am no actor, and that I cannot attempt a convincing Ulster accent in public does not prevent me from realising the characters and the scene. I am able to place an accent in my mind upon the speech. More demanding by far is the need to respond to the various characters in this poem. I can manage the narrator who, in any case, remains quite neutral; so neutral, in fact, that his distance from the actions becomes an important element in the creation of an innocent viewpoint in the poem. It is important, too, with regard to the function of irony. That irony is what makes the ending of this poem so critical; the priest's tone of voice and the emphasis which Paul Muldoon's punctuation imposes on the exchange between the young girl in the confessional and the spiritual 'Father' is a challenge to the reader. I have read the poem 'aloud' twice now and am favouring a softer, perhaps insidious tone for the priest, rather than a sternly authoritarian one. I read the final line with the sense of the girl's shyness, and yet with a defensive wonderment in the last 'Very gently'. Certainly, these lines occasion more deliberation than the clear-cut and rather futile blustering of the father with his amusing comments on Kennedy.

3   *What patterns can I see in the poem?*

The poem is firmly divided into three verses, though there is no rhyme-scheme. The first verse comes the closest to establishing a pattern with several rhyming words – 'morning / nothing', 'you are / bother', as well as the internal near-rhyme of 'at war' with 'bother'. In verse two the local accent would pull together 'Armagh' and 'better', closer perhaps than a 'received' English accent might. There is, too, the consonant rhyme of 'word / mind / God', but this does not really constitute an important patterning effect, other than the weighty sense of responsibility which her father wishes to impose upon May. In the third verse the third and fourth lines end with 'once' and line 17 also repeats the word so that we have it three times. Paul Muldoon is underlining the uniqueness and importance of the experience for the girl. To that end the last three lines slow down the pace; the words come in their own time as both priest and 'sinner' reach towards the fact of the 'sin'. Here we see that 'immodest . . . breast' and 'me . . . he . . . he . . . me . . . gently' softly insist the fact of the sexual encounter.

The organisation of the poem into three verses is the most important aspect of the poet's strategy in the text. The first verse introduces, albeit obliquely, the protagonists. May, as yet unnamed, is the main subject of the poem, though her father, directly, and her brother or sister, the narrator, indirectly, are located cleverly and with great economy simply by the inferences and the drama of the situation. Paul Muldoon is making his reader work right from the start and this is a positive strength in the poem. We as readers are engaged in the creative act from the very beginning and so are prepared to involve our imaginative responses in the process of decoding the text. For this is a text which requires our active participation, it seems to me. The first two verses are dominated by the father, his bluster and the unconscious humour in his terms of expression. The two worlds of the household and family and the wider world of international affairs and the Cold War are both implicated and set against each other in those first two verses. In the last verse the focus narrows and, paradoxically, deepens. The brother, Paul Muldoon perhaps (for we have no reason to suppose that the narrator is any other), reports on the conversation he hears from the other side of the confessional curtain. The confessional is a place which excludes everything apart from words. It is the theatre of language *par excellence*. There are no possibilities for body language; one's whole being has to be expressed through diction, syntax, the pacing and pausing of one's words. There are just four lines of authorial comment, of physical placing, in this poem, and they are quite neutral. Both the first and last verse are briefly introduced; the second verse is prepared for by the father's pounding of the table at the end of the first verse. But it is as if even that bareness of narrative is whittled away as the poem moves towards the characters' own struggle with the world through language.

4   *Discuss any ambiguities or paradoxes in the poem.*

As we may now be expecting, the title of this poem presents the first dilemma. The action is clearly not set in an island in the Carribean, nor is it concerned with that island beyond the fact that in our recent history the concern of the whole world became focused on that island and the attempt of its president, Fidel Castro, to site Russian nuclear missiles there. Cuba is as

close to the southern tip of the USA as Britain is to the Channel
Islands, so an international incident developed which escalated
to the point of a nuclear 'showdown' between the USA and the
USSR. Some readers might not remember the details of that des-
perately dangerous time, but I think it is reasonable to suppose
that most readers of this poem would be triggered by the words
of the father into locating what is, after all, the most critically
threatening international incident of the last 40 years.

I have already pointed out that readers are forced to make
connections for themselves as far as the location and relationships
in this poem are concerned. Phrases such as 'With the world at
war, if not at an end', 'Those Yankees were touch and go' and
'Patton at Armagh' might well prove perplexing taken in isolation.
The poem comes into being only when the reader has brought
these elements into a meaningful whole. Again, when faced by a
confusing text, we must constantly return to a reading of the piece
and rest on the common sense assumption that the writer has a
clear purpose. Certainly, within the context of academic study and
the examination system this is always the case and our faith will
always have been justified. In any case, *Cuba* opens with such an
obvious conviction of detail that we do accept the credibility of
the events. The father's outburst is so true to life, isn't it? He sees
May as wearing 'next to nothing'; it's all a 'bother' and President
Kennedy has 'only to say the word'. The colloquial manner of
the speech encourages the reader to bear with the limitations in
understanding and articulation of the speaker, and, too, with the
self-deprecating humour of

> But this Kennedy's nearly an Irishman
> So he's not much better than ourselves.

The various nations of the UK have, as we discussed in the
analysis of Fred D'Aguiar's poem, particular accents that lend
speech and writing special possibilities of cadence, rhythm and
emphasis. Anger or excitement in a character will exaggerate
those qualities. In *Cuba* May's father is angry, with some justification, but his anger hovers between fear and absurdity. In the
context of the Cuba missile crisis, the misdemeanour of his daughter is trivial: in the context of their family life it is of considerable
importance. It marks the transition from child to adult; May is
beginning to move away from the protection of the home and is

touching on experiences which are adult and necessary. However, such experiences frequently occasion pain and misunderstanding, both for parents and their children. To understand the poem we must listen carefully to the speech of the father and understand the tension he feels, both at the family level, and in the wider context of the very real threat to world peace. His engagement with the first, albeit in a rather conventional and clumsy way, is going some way towards compensating for the fact that he can do nothing about the second, larger issue.

The second verse underlines this fact very cleverly by its confusion of the two issues. The father has moved from May's behaviour to the missile crisis, to a digression concerning the character and antecedents of President Kennedy. He returns to the problem of his daughter with the last sentence of the second verse. The world is in such a turmoil and May has put herself in such mortal danger by her sinning that a commitment to the confessional would appear to be the only solution. This is, after all, a devoutly Catholic household.

The change of scene, intensity of focus and pace in the final verse has the effect, almost, of a film's cutting. There is an injection of drama simply by the act of plunging the reader into a different scene. This rapid change may well throw some readers off balance for a moment, but Paul Muldoon is obviously intending that we should juxtapose the father's dilemma with his proposed 'solution'. This short poem has moved concisely over three important subjects: the development of an individual within a family, the Cold War in the decades following the Second World War and the Roman Catholic Church. Of course, that is a crude and simplistic summary, for the poem is addressing those issues primarily and essentially through its portrayal of people and their emotions. This is most acutely demonstrated by the confessional scene. The relationship between the priest and the girl should be that of a professional man of God giving advice to a confused adolescent. It is, however, profoundly ambiguous. It may well be important to his analysis that he elicits details of May's 'sin' from her, but it is also implied by the pace and emphasis of his words that his interest might well be the source of excitation. His concern may, in fact, be the prurient interest of a frustrated man. That would be the ultimate irony, wouldn't it? May's father, in his concern for her and his reliance on the Church, has himself been naïve, perhaps.

There is one further possibility. May's final words, the last line of the poem, allow one to see her as coming to a realisation for herself. Again, the pace and emphasis of those words do allow for her remembrance of the physical sensation of the 'sin'. She has enjoyed the strangeness of another's touch and has sensed in that contact, paradoxically, the suggestion of a respect for her as a person which is as real as the more obvious actions of her family and certainly of more consequence than the questioning of the priest.

> He brushed against me, Father. Very gently.

Her use of 'brushed' is significant. It is not simply a 'touch', far less a caress, though those possibilities are contained in the word, especially when it is qualified by the distinction 'Very gently'. That comes as both an afterthought and a justification of her right as an individual to experience. The implication is that May has a real need of touch; she needs contact outside the family and the Church if she is to grow beyond their protection and constraints and become herself. The three sins she recites

> I told a lie once, I was disobedient once,
> And, Father, a boy touched me once.

disguise by their rote the truth that all three are the same experience won against the odds during her night out. Through the ritual of the confessional the subtext has become text.

5 *Summarise my responses to the poem.*

Paul Muldoon's Cuba engages the reader's interest and imagination at several levels. It succeeds in relating the concerns of personal and family life to larger and less tangible political issues. Whilst acknowledging that, for most of us, the perspective will always be limited by our immediate experience and concern for people close to us, the poet convincingly underlines the fact that it is from such personal concerns that the world must ultimately advance. It is imperative that May's father should talk to his daughter just as it is vital that Kennedy and Krushchev resolve their strategical tensions by negotiation. At the same time, it is clear that the world is a complex place and that people may not be all that they appear to be. Even a priest can be subject to motivations which cloud his judgement and warp his behaviour. The Church itself may play an ambiguous role in both personal and larger affairs.

We associate very closely with May and her predicament as she finds herself subject to the voices of male authority both of her father and of the priest. It is the same kind of abuse of masculine power that has brought about the political crisis from which the poem takes its name. It is deeply ironical that it should take the tension of a world crisis to illuminate the importance of personal honesty, both between people and with regard to a person's own view of themselves. Adolescents often act impulsively because they do not realise that life is indeed long enough for them to work out their own terms. That pressure to act, to take hold on experience is also present when peaceful stability is threatened. May's family feel the strain of the possible nuclear holocaust and are especially mindful of their spiritual state. So, *Cuba* succeeds in raising profound questions about personal morality and the role of the Church. But Paul Muldoon's major achievement is in the manner in which he engages the reader: it is concise, moving, entertaining and philosophical at once. We, as readers, are effectively drawn into a dramatic situation and then, as with all truly successful works of art, we are challenged to consider our own solution to the dilemma.

7

Writing an analysis

THIS book has stressed the importance of a positive, questioning approach to poetry because that is the key both to enjoying poetry and also to successful examination and assignment work. Faced by a poem new to us we should regard the experience of reading the text as similar to that of meeting a person for the first time: there should be a sense of expectancy at the possibility of a new relationship and this should override any feelings of wariness we might have. What are we to learn from the poem? What does it hold for us? And what will it expect from us in return? Remember that teachers and examiners are concerned not to baffle and defeat students: their aim is to introduce students to new experiences which extend their perceptions and encourage them to develop their reading skills.

The five steps which I have used in forming my responses to the poems studied in this book provide you with a basic framework for analysing a text. That framework can also form the foundation of a written response both to poems encountered as part of a larger study of a poet, theme or period, and to poems presented as an unseen text in an examination or an assignment. Having a framework like this will help you to keep your confidence in the face of texts that are new to you, and possibly threatening because they are unfamiliar. However, my guidelines, or for that matter anybody else's guidelines, should be regarded as flexible; they are to support and guide you, not to shackle you to a straight and narrow track. You will have noticed that in tackling some poems, for example, Dylan Thomas's *A Refusal to Mourn* or Sylvia Plath's *Daddy*, the first step, *What kind of writing is shaped in front of me?* leads to a brief and obvious response. The fact that I have stated the obvious – length, number and regularity of verses – does serve to establish in my mind the overall structure of the poem. As we have seen, structure, on the page and within individual lines, is of the greatest importance in poetry. These are the factors which most obviously make poetry what it is; they distinguish poetry from prose. That does not mean to say, however, that we should necessarily open our written response to a poem by stating those facts. We may wish instead to respond immediately to a poem's theme or use of persona. Sometimes, however, it will be the case that the very shape and appearance of the poem offers a challenge to our conceptions of poetry, and in that instance we will have to deal with the innovations and deliberate challenges that the poet has laid down on the page before us. I am thinking here of poems such as those by William Carlos Williams. You are unlikely to be asked to write about concrete poems as such, but you may well come across poems from the 'Black Mountain Poets' or Lawrence Ferlinghetti from America, or poems by Edwin Morgan, the Scottish poet who has employed such strategies to good effect. His *The Computer's First Christmas Card*, for example, has been widely anthologised. The American e. e. cummings is also widely published in anthologies in Britain. His use of words in a way that flows down a page and his individualistic use of capitals and punctuation (which, as you see, extended even to his name) demand that readers respond to the shape of the poem on the page. It is really from these examples of the extreme use of physical structure that I have taken my lead. However, all poems, even poems more conventionally presented, are distinguished from other forms of writing essentially by their appearance on the page and, therefore, that is always likely to influence our initial response.

Timing

It is vitally important in any examination to organise your time effectively. Allow time to read and reread the poem, sounding out its tone and pace and emphases. It can be very useful to make notes and markings – arrows, circles, underlinings – on the text itself as a guide to instances of the poet's techniques and patterns as you perceive them.

Whether your task is an essay or a timed question, the time you spend on planning your writing is always time well spent. Defining your response and outlining *for yourself* the intention and strategies of the poet as you see them will lead you to write a better analysis. So many students fail to do themselves justice in examinations because they begin to write without first forming a clear idea of the points they want to make and the end-point they wish to reach in their essay. If you are writing a course-work essay which covers more than one poem from a poet or number of poets, then you will probably not have the space or time to analyse each poem in the sort of detail which we have given to most of the poems in this book. Your choice of poems for analysis from a wider range of work will hold the key to your success if those study poems have not already been specified. Personal taste will play a part then, but there is also the need to respond to a representative range of poems in order to deal with the poet's themes and variations of style and strategy. Obviously, the time and length of writing which you allow respective poems will give the clearest indication of the relative importance in which you hold them. If you run out of time in an examination make sure that you indicate briefly the direction and purpose of those paragraphs which you had intended to write. But the sensible student does not run out of time: she or he is sufficiently in control of the question, and is sufficiently aware of the overall length and shape of their written answer, to gauge the time correctly. If you know what you are doing and set about the task confidently, you will be able to do what is required in the available time.

Themes and answers

If you are answering a set question, then make sure that you answer the demands of *that* question. Do not attempt to offload everything that you know about a poet and the poems you have studied. All the material you use should be addressed to the demands of the question. In order to ensure your material is relevant, it is always a good idea to question the question itself because that will make you focus on the specific demands of that question.

For example, how might we respond if asked to discuss the following question: 'Alun Lewis's work is "not merely an expression of the conflicts within his world, but itself a new direction through the deep."' Well, the key points here would seem to be 'conflicts within his world' and 'a new direction through the deep'. We will obviously have to examine and try to explain the nature of the conflicts which we think the poet deals with. Then we must decide whether these conflicts are strictly speaking of 'his world', or whether they are dilemmas which Lewis shares with other human beings. If the poet deals only with those conflicts within himself, and specific to his situation, then at what point may we be encouraged to empathise with him? Why should we care? We must ask ourselves whether the moral and emotional dilemmas which a young man faces at the onset of war when his ideals are centred on love and peace can engage us and be instructive for our lives. Then we must turn to the question of whether the poet points towards a 'new direction' through the depth of his concern and confusion about the meaning of life. In what way can a poem be itself an act which positively moves the poet and the reader towards a deeper understanding and a clearer course of action? If we were simply examining *All Day it has Rained* in the light of this remark, then we might argue that a sense of foreboding, even fatalism, descends upon Lewis at the end of the poem and that it doesn't point in a 'new direction'. However, taking into account the context of futile inactivity and boredom which the poet has so convincingly created in the poem, we might well see that fatalism as a passing mood and wish to consider further poems before coming to a firm conclusion about the overall impact of Lewis's work and its direction.

If, after several readings of an unseen poem, you remain confused or unsure about any aspect of it, be honest, confront the fact of your insecurity and try to turn that into a positive response by explaining the nature and the degree of your confusion. Remember, some poems are difficult because of the nature of the experience the poet is trying to write about, such as love, mortality, the death of a loved one, the sense of alienation in an unfriendly environment, the incidence of racial abuse, the cruelty of human beings to animals and their fellow human-beings. None of these things is easily written about, and yet poets must continue to address these facts and by their skill offer new approaches to these problems. Remember, poets are not politicians or preachers; their approach will probably be less direct, more oblique, more suggestive of the complexity of the factors involved. Also, examiners will tend to respond to what they recognise as your genuine, if still exploratory, approach to an unseen poem.

The language of poetry

Be aware of the effects of prosody – the poet's special way with words and the relationships between words: diction, syntax, metaphor, rhyme, imperfect rhyme, rhythm, caesura or line pause, run-on lines and verse structures. But do try and talk about these in as natural a way as possible, using your analysis of such effects as a means of explaining the poem's effect on you and contributing naturally to your interpretation of the poem's meaning. Do not simply present a list of such effects as if you were spotting trains or birds. Always comment in detail on particular aspects of imagery and language. Say precisely why they strike you as interesting and how they make a contribution to the overall effect and intention of the poem. Look back, for example, at my treatment of the sounds and images in Seamus Heaney's *Death of a Naturalist* under steps 3 and 4 at the beginning of Chapter 5.

However, don't quote from the poem unless there is a good reason. (This is, of course, particularly the case when you are dealing with an unseen poem printed before you on an examination paper.) Remember, if you quote you must comment on the special qualities of those particular words which you have chosen to highlight in this way or you will have wasted precious time and space in your answer. For this reason it is likely that your quotations will be relatively short.

When you are discussing the broader effects of a poet's work, or comparing and contrasting the work of a number of poets, then try to connect your arguments by specific reference to the *language* of the poet. It is the words on the page that finally determine the effect and achieve the intention of the poet. However, in an examination, if you forget some of your chosen quotations or become slightly confused under the pressure of the situation, again, don't panic! Use as much of those quotations which illustrate special devices of language, diction, syntax, imagery, as you can recall. Remember, examinations are not primarily concerned with testing your memory. It is ideas for which the examiner is looking. But it is better to support your argument by even a small phrase than to give no point of reference at all in the text. *Half a line is better than none.* But remember, the real point of quoting is to support your argument, not to show you have learnt the text parrot-fashion.

Conclusion

Make sure that you end your essay or answer with a paragraph which draws together the main elements of your response and which emphasises your personal feelings about the poem. The overall effect of your answer, whether in an examination or an essay, should be that of developing an argument or point of view. You must try and convince the marker that you are working towards a summary of your personal, but considered responses because, in the end, it is *your* response, the unique relationship, between you and the writer, you and the poem, which is the whole point of your writing, and the whole point of English Literature as a subject for study.

Here is a summary of the main points for you to remember:

1 **Read through unseen poems carefully** trying to hear the sounds and patterns which the poet has created.
2 **Question the question** and try to get clear in your mind precisely what it requires of you.
3 **Note the main features and make a paragraph plan** using diagrammatic marks on the text itself in order to locate patterns and highlight interesting aspects of language or form.
4 **Begin your responses in a direct and positive way**: for example, by addressing the question or, if it is an unseen poetry criticism, the theme of the poem.
5 **Draw your response to a conclusion** even if you have honestly to confront the fact that some aspects of the poem still elude you.

One last point: many poems are presented in stanzas or verses – separate units, each with a kind of integrity and coherence of its own. Why not think of the structure of your essays in a similar way? After an introductory paragraph, each paragraph of your essay or answer should be a clear unit that advances the case. If you are discussing an unseen poem of four verses, for example, your essay might have an opening paragraph and a closing paragraph, and then four central paragraphs each devoted to one of the verses of the poem. The point I am making is that, not only is the structure of the poem on the page important, the structure of your essay is also important, that it must build a response in clearly defined paragraph steps. That will provide you with a disciplined and organised framework, in which you might well surprise yourself at just how many perceptive ideas you can produce about the poem or poet you are studying.

Further reading

The most useful preparation for dealing with the poetry demands of your English Literature course is to read as much and as varied poetry as you can. The more you read, the less likely it is that you will be faced by a poem which baffles you by its diction, form or imagery. This reading does not have to lead to a written response anymore than an evening's viewing of the television or a film leads necessarily to a review column in the morning's newspaper. There is no reason why the reading of poetry should not fulfil the sort of function which a paperback novel might do. Poetry books are invariably paperbacks too; they contain the sort of writing which is short and concentrated – ideal for periodic, even casual reading matter. Poems can work rather like short stories, or the short chapters of a novel, building up an impression of the world as portrayed by a single person with an unique vision. Try reading, for example, Philip Larkin's collection *The Whitsun Weddings*, from which the poem *The Whitsun Weddings* was taken. That collection works in such a way. So do Sylvia Plath's *Ariel*, Ted Hughes's *Crow* and, more recently, Douglas Dunn's *Elegies*, Craig Raine's *The Martian Sends a Postcard Home* and Dannie Abse's *Ask the Bloody Horse*.

I have listed further collected works below along with some anthologies that you may find interesting, together with some critical books. In addition, as you will see, I have included a few brief biographical notes on those poets I have discussed in case you wish to know more about them.

Criticism

The Practice of Poetry (Heinemann, 1971), by Robin Skelton and *The Poet's Craft* (Heinemann, 1975), again by Robin Skelton, are very readable books concerned with the role and working practices of poets. Skelton, himself a poet, writes in an enthusiastic and accessible way. *The Poet's Manual and Rhyming Dictionary* by Frances Stillman (Thames and Hudson, 1976) is still the most useful handbook for those who practise both poetry and criticism. Again, the Open University booklets on specific periods or movements are very useful. See, for example, the course books on *Modernism* or T. S. Eliot. The Macmillan Casebook series is also excellent and includes several volumes which deal with major poets of the early and mid-twentieth century.

As far as post-war poets are concerned there are a number of studies which deal with the poets we've looked at including, *Poetry in the Wars* by Edna Longley (Bloodaxe Books, 1986), *The Art of the Real: Poetry in England and America since 1939* by Eric Homburger (Dent, 1977) and *British Poetry Since 1960: a critical survey*, edited by Michael Schmidt and Grevel Lindop (Carcanet Press, 1972).

Anthologies

The Penguin Book of Contemporary British Poetry, eds Blake Morrison and Andrew Motion (Penguin, 1982).

The Oxford Book of Twentieth Century Verse, chosen by Philip Larkin (O.U.P., 1973). It is interesting to compare this with the earlier *Oxford Book* by W. B. Yeats.

British Poetry since 1945, ed. Edward Lucie-Smith (Penguin, 1970).

Poetry of the Forties, ed. Robin Skelton (Penguin, 1968).

The New Poetry, ed. A. Alvarez (Penguin 1966).

The Penguin Book of American Verse, ed. Geoffrey Moore (Penguin, 1977).

Contemporary American Poetry, ed. Donald Hall (Penguin, 1972).

The Faber Book of Twentieth Century Women's Poetry, ed. Fleur Adcock (Faber, 1987).

The Faber Book of Contemporary Irish Poetry, ed. Paul Muldoon (Faber & Faber, 1986).

Anglo-Welsh Poetry 1480–1980, eds R. Garlick and R. Mathias (Poetry Wales Press, 1984).

Twelve Modern Scottish Poets, eds C. King and I. C. Smith (Hodder, 1986).

Individual poets

WILLIAM CARLOS WILLIAMS (1883–1963)

An American who determined to write an especially new and 'American' poetry. His long poem *Paterson* is set in the New England town where he practised as a doctor.

1 TEXTS
Selected Poems (Penguin Books, 1976).

2 CRITICISM
William Carlos Williams in *The Critical Heritage Series*, ed. Doyle (Routledge & Kegan Paul, 1980).

ADRIENNE RICH

Born 1929. One of the leading American poets, having won many notable literary awards. An anti-Vietnam War activist, she now lives in New England where she runs a radical feminist press.

1 TEXTS
Selected Poems (Norton, New York, 1975).
Blood, Bread and Poetry, prose and criticism (Virago, 1987).

2 CRITICISM
Adrienne Rich's Poetry, eds B. Gelpi and A. Gelpi (Norton, New York, 1980).

TONY CURTIS

Born 1946, Carmarthen. Teaches literature and creative writing at the Polytechnic of Wales.

TEXTS
Selected Poems 1970–1985 (Poetry Wales Press, 1986).
The Last Candles (Seren Books, 1989).

ALUN LEWIS (1915–44)

Born in Cwmamman, in the south Wales coalfield. He was one of the best poets of the Second World War. He was not conscripted, but left his schoolteacher's position to enlist in 1940. He was subsequently commissioned and served with the South Wales Borderers in Burma and India. He was killed as result of a shot from his revolver.

TEXTS
Selected Poems, eds J. Hooker and Gweno Lewis (Allen & Unwin, 1981).
Alun Lewis: A Miscellany of his writings, ed. John Pikoulis (Poetry Wales Press, 1982).

KEITH DOUGLAS (1920–44)

Born in Tunbridge Wells. Like Lewis, he is regarded as one of the finest war poets and, like Lewis, he was commissioned and chose to go into the front line. He saw action as a tank commander in North Africa (see *Alamein to Zem Zem*). His *Selected Poems* were published just before his death in the Normandy campaign.

1 TEXTS
Complete Poems, ed. Desmond Graham (O.U.P., 1987).
Keith Douglas: A Prose Miscellany, ed. Desmond Graham (Carcanet Press, 1985).

2 CRITICISM
Keith Douglas 1920–1944: A Biography, by Desmond Graham (O.U.P., 1974).

DYLAN THOMAS (1914–53)

Worked as a journalist in his home town of Swansea and as a broadcaster in London. Known for his experiments in verse and his magnificently dramatic readings. Much of his fame and money was earned as a result of poetry reading tours of America. Many recordings exist and hearing Thomas himself reading *Refusal to Mourn* would greatly assist your understanding of the poem and encourage you to tackle such difficult poems with greater confidence.

1 TEXTS
Collected Poems, 1934–1953 (Dent, 1988).

2 CRITICISM
Dylan Thomas, by Walford Davies (O.U.P., 1986).

R. S. THOMAS

Born in Cardiff in 1913. He entered the Church in Wales and was a priest in rural and north Wales until his retirement in 1983. His range is wide and continues to shift in focus, from the early poems about the communities he served, on to Welsh nationalist politics and protests as well as ecological and anti-nuclear work.

1 TEXTS

Selected Poems 1946–1968 (Bloodaxe Books, 1986).
R. S. Thomas: Selected Prose, ed. Sandra Anstey (Poetry Wales Press, 1986).

2 CRITICISM

Critical Writings on R. S. Thomas, ed. Sandra Anstey (Poetry Wales Press, 1982).

PHILIP LARKIN (1922–86)

Born in Coventry (see the poem *I Remember, I Remember.*) He is one of the most significant of post-war poets in Britain. He worked for many years as Librarian at the University of Hull and was also a jazz critic for *The Daily Telegraph*. He wrote two novels, but his reputation rests principally on the four collections of poems which are now collected in a single volume. *The Whitsun Weddings* and *High Windows* are, arguably, the strongest, most unified collections of poetry to appear in Britain since the war.

1 TEXTS

Collected Poems, ed. Anthony Thwaite (Faber & Faber, 1988).

2 CRITICISM

Philip Larkin, by Andrew Motion (Methuen, 1982).
Philip Larkin, by Roger Day (Open University Press, 1976).

TED HUGHES

Born 1930 in Yorkshire. He came to prominence in the late 1950s and secured a large reputation with collections such as *Woodwo*, *Lupercal* and the remarkable *Crow*; which reworked the genesis myth, incorporating a cartoon-like characterisation of a crow. He is now a farmer in Devon as well as being our Poet Laureate. His first wife was Sylvia Plath.

1 TEXTS
Selected Poems 1957–1981 (Faber & Faber, 1982).

2 CRITICISM
The Achievement of Ted Hughes, ed. Keith Sagar (Manchester University Press, 1987).

SYLVIA PLATH (1932–63)

Born in Boston where she had early success as a student and as a writer. She then studied at Cambridge where she met Ted Hughes. They were married and had two children. Tragically, she committed suicide in 1963. Ted Hughes edited her unpublished poems (she was writing many in her final months) and they were published posthumously as the collection *Ariel*.

1 TEXTS
Collected Poems, (Faber & Faber, 1981).
The Bell Jar, a novel, (Faber & Faber, 1967).

2 CRITICISM
Sylvia Plath, by Susan Bassnett (*Women Writers Series*, Macmillan, 1987).
Sylvia Plath, ed. L. Wagner (*Critical Heritage Series*, Routledge & Kegan Paul, 1988).

SEAMUS HEANEY

Born in Belfast in 1938. His reputation is now paramount among contemporary poets from the British Isles. His early poems about growing up in a rural area in Northern Ireland, of which *Death of a Naturalist* is a notable example, have continued into later collections. Heaney has also come to deal with the Irish Troubles. His poetry is more frequently specifically political, and, given the continuing political tension in that island, much of his work may now be seen as relevant to that wider context.

1 TEXTS
Selected Poems 1965–1972 (Faber & Faber, 1980).
Preoccupations: Selected Prose 1968–78 (Faber & Faber, 1980).

2 CRITICISM

The Art of Seamus Heaney, ed. Tony Curtis (Poetry Wales Press & Dufour Editions, 1986).
Seamus Heaney by Blake Morrison (Methuen, 1982).
Seamus Heaney by Neil Cocoran (Faber & Faber, 1986).

LESLIE NORRIS

Born on a farm near Merthyr Tydfil in south Wales in 1921. He has published a number of collections of poetry and two collections of short stories.

TEXTS

Selected Poems (Poetry Wales Press, 1986).
The Girl from Cardigan, stories (Seren Books, 1988).

DANNIE ABSE

Born in Cardif in 1923. He qualified as a doctor at the end of the Second World War and practised at a chest clinic in London for many years whilst also working as a writer and as a frequent broadcaster. He is President of The Poetry Society in the U.K.

1 TEXTS

White Coat, Purple Coat, Collected Poems, 1948–1988 (Hutchinson, 1989).
Ash on a Young Man's Sleeve, an autobiographical novel (Penguin Books, 1982).

2 CRITICISM

The Poetry of Dannie Abse, ed. Joseph Cohen (Robson Books, 1983).
Dannie Abse, by Tony Curtis (University of Wales Press, 1985).

FRED D'AGUIAR

Born in 1960 in London of Guyanese parents, but was brought up in Guyana. He completed his secondary education in London, trained as psychiatric nurse, then read English and did postgraduate work at the University of Kent. His first book was well received.

TEXT

Mama Dot (Chatto & Windus, 1985).

GILLIAN CLARKE

Born in Cardiff in 1937. She began to publish when she was 33, after raising a family. She now lives principally in rural west Wales, in a cottage called 'Blaen Cwrt', about which she has written a poem which sets the keynote for her celebration of nature and her return to the everyday language of Welsh. She is probably the most active visiting poet in British schools and colleges.

1 TEXTS
Selected Poems (Carcanet, 1985).
Letting in the Rumour (Carcanet, 1989).

2 CRITICISM
Chapter 13 'Big Sea Running in the Shell', in *The Presence of the Past*, by Jeremy Hooker (Seren Books, 1989).

PAUL MULDOON

Born in 1951 in County Armagh in Northern Ireland. He worked as a producer for the BBC in Belfast, but presently lives in New York. He is regarded as the most notable of a number of poets from Northern Ireland to emulate Seamus Heaney's success.

1 TEXTS
Selected Poems (Faber & Faber, 1986).
Meeting the British (Faber & Faber, 1987).

2 CRITICISM
Poetry in the Wars by Edna Longley (Bloodaxe, 1986).